Can You Hear Me Now?

THE STORY OF AN UNLIKELY INVITATION

JAKE MORAN

WWW.UNLIKELYINVITATION.COM

WESTBOW®
PRESS
A DIVISION OF THOMAS NELSON
& ZONDERVAN

WestBow Press books may be ordered through booksellers or by contacting:

WestBow Press
A Division of Thomas Nelson & Zondervan
1663 Liberty Drive
Bloomington, IN 47403
www.westbowpress.com
1 (866) 928-1240

ISBN: 978-1-4908-3111-4 (sc)
ISBN: 978-1-4908-3112-1 (hc)
ISBN: 978-1-4908-3110-7 (e)
Library of Congress Control Number: 2014905433

Printed in the United States of America.

WestBow Press rev. date: 04/21/2014

PREFACE

I am a sinner.

But this is not, at the core, a story about Jake from Georgia.

It's a story about Jesus from Nazareth... never leaving the equation of life, regardless of the season, valley, or mountain you are experiencing.

It's a glimpse at the raw reality of my life, for better or worse... through better and worse, with an unfading and unfailing God... so that people who have never seen Jesus... can see Jesus.

ACKNOWLEDGEMENTS

This isn't the kind of 'acknowledgements' bit that you see on Oscar's night. It's far more personal than that. I guess I would just like to acknowledge that there are far too many people involved in my life to 'thank' or list for their support and involvement in all that has gone on the over the course of this story.

True friendship is a dwindling commodity it seems; the call to genuine friendship exists in the rare form of people being the kind of friend they desire to have... and doing it consistently. This has been one of those seasons in life where, though the circumstances are not ideal, you have the opportunity to see the depth and quality of the friendships and relationships you have developed with others.

During the first few weeks of the story you are about to read, I think I paid for three meals. "Overwhelmed" cannot begin to describe the level of gratitude and humility I felt as I seemingly had people coming out of the woodwork to have me over for dinner after work, send an invite for a cup of coffee, meet up for lunch, shoot me random text messages of encouragement and support... over and over and over again.

For those of you, that know who you are, I will, for the rest of my life, be humbled by the tangible nature of your love, friendship, and support. Tears of gratitude fill my eyes even as I write this and travel back in time to those first few weeks.

You are treasured.

INTRODUCTION

This is an admittedly abnormal book.

To confess, I'm not sure if I can legitimately call this a 'book'. Someone who read an earlier draft told me I should write an actual introduction… that's how much I really didn't consider it a book; it took someone else to state the obvious I guess? This is probably more of a chronicle than anything else. The events and instances recorded in what you're about to read are as accurate as I can describe them and recall them. I've tried to keep things free from embellishment, because the reality is this: when God is involved in the story, you just don't need to do a whole lot more than write it down.

A number of people that have read earlier versions of this have all had the same initial comment; "I started reading and couldn't put it down." This is not my doing. This is a story God has written (and is continuing to write); my fingers simply did the typing. But in light of some of the feedback, I guess I should say this in advance… don't start reading this with your kids or pets still in the car.

If nothing else comes of this, I hope you will see with a new degree of clarity, as I have, that Jesus' words "…and surely I am with you always, to the very end of the age (Matthew 28:20 NIV)" are as relevant today as they were two thousand years ago. He is the King of and through the valleys of life… just as much as He is King of and over life's peaks. This story takes you through the full terrain of my life, good and bad, with a God who is always near.

In the Old Testament, Job records a conversation he has with God in which God asks Job who he thinks waters a land where no man lives or a desert with no one in it (Job 38:26)? Why would God water a land with no life around it? Because He is always doing things on purpose, for a purpose… to prepare the ground for our arrival.

I have become abundantly aware that the ways and workings of God are so far outside my field of vision it's comical to think I will ever 'get' Him. God does and is doing things 'behind the curtain of life' of which I cannot see, therefore cannot fully understand. I love Job 38 because it *begins with this*… "Then the Lord answered Job out of the storm."

Sometimes, it seems, God allows a storm to intersect our lives in order to communicate more easily… directly… with us; so we can hear His voice with greater clarity.

There are three songs that I will share over the course of this book, each intersecting my life for the very first time at a critical place in the life of this story. Each song is kind of an anthem of what I was going through, or launching into, as it relates to this journey with God; I guess that's why they are so memorable and were so encouraging… and why I choose to share them with you. Due to the expense of copyright permissions, I can't publish the full lyrics, so I'd encourage you to look them up online.

The first is a song that, through the first few months of this story, I sang and cried along with nearly every day on the way to and from work. I'm not exaggerating. I listened to Matt Redman's "10,000 Reasons" album every day for a solid three months straight and could not make it through the drive to or from my office without tears running down my face. It was the only thing in my CD player for at least 90 days straight.

But this one song stood apart from the others. I would daily speak its truth, though my circumstances wanted to dictate a vastly different state of affairs. I hope and pray, as you read through this story, that you will see our God…

… can be trusted.

… walks with us.

… fights for us.

… is faithful.

Matt Redman "Never Once"
from the *10,000 Reasons* Album (2012)

Standing on this mountaintop
Looking just how far we've come
Knowing that for every step
You were with us

...

Heck, this isn't really much of an 'introduction'. All I can say is I hope you enjoy the ride.

Our God never sleeps.

So here we go...

1

UNINTENDED

I had no intention of ever writing this. I had no intention of any of this ever happening. Yet, as I try to recall all that God has done over the pages you are about to read, I am amazed. *Stupefied* is probably a more apt word. I catch myself over and over again just shaking my head in absolute disbelief and wonder. God is so incredible.

So much has happened that, as I read through my journal of the events that have transpired, I realize I've forgotten a good bit already. The God activity has been so frequent and crazy that a lot of the small stuff has dropped off the memory train. Thank goodness for having a journal.

For reasons I could not understand or explain, in early November of 2012 (about three months in) I felt distinctly impressed to begin writing this story out. I really had no idea -- no clue whatsoever -- as to why I felt this prodding within me to start typing this into my computer. It was maybe ten-to-fifteen pages or so at that point. I remember thinking numerous times, "What on earth am I going to do with this?!" Now I understand why I was supposed to start writing then (as you preview the current page count).

I've never done anything remotely like this or to this extent before. Sharing this level of detail is, frankly, *really* uncomfortable... and it's rather embarrassing in some places too. Honestly, revealing some of my hurt, faults, and "special-needs" faith adds an extra level of "awkward" for me on top of everything else. But as it's become clear to me, while this intimately involves me, this story is not about me. A friend of mine told me a few months into this story, "Regardless of what happens, God is going to get glory in your life." And that is the absolute truth. So my hope and prayer is that somehow, someway, God will use this (whatever 'this' is) to bring glory to Himself.

To some, even after reading this, you may still question my judgment or think this is somewhat far-fetched. To some extent, I would honestly have to agree. This is far-fetched... but I'm not the one writing the story; I'm just doing a lot of typing. If that's you, my questions would simply be, "What else can you make of this? What other conclusion can you reach?" If you can come up with an answer, I'd love to know. I can't come up with a single one.

A number of people who have read through this book (some of whom have walked through this story with me) have said to me that they had to go back and read it again... because they just can't believe the series of events that have unfolded. Having shared this story with one of my best friends, he simply said, "You know what I love most about this story? It's that most people, even a lot of Christians, believe that stories like this are 'from days of old' -- they don't believe stuff like this happens anymore -- they don't believe God interacts and speaks and moves in the lives of ordinary people. That's what makes this story so great."

This friend, a true brother in the faith (and in life in general), is one of my most treasured relationships, and is a voice I allow to freely speak into my life for two very unique reasons.

The first: he genuinely loves Jesus.

The second: he is not impressed with me or anything about me.

These are the types of relationships that make me feel like a rich man.

The ensuing pages are, effectively, my transcription and description of the majority of what I've tracked in my journal and what has occurred outside its front and back cover. It's not every single thing that's happened, but it's enough.

It is God's beckoning call to me and His reaffirming summons on my life:

"Son, can you hear Me now?"

2

THE DAY

Saturday, August 4, 2012

To quote FDR, "A day that will live in infamy" -- in my life at least.

It was the day my wife and I came home from our last counseling session. She had decided she was leaving.

I listened to my life slowly shatter into little pieces around my living room. I knew things had not been good. Two sinners living in close proximity to each other tends to yield some conflict and adversity; we definitely had our share. There were a number of things I wished I'd done differently and some other things I felt like I had flat out failed at. The apostle Paul describes in 1 Corinthians 13 that our ability to love -- to see love in its purest form (this side of Heaven) -- is like looking into a dim or dirty mirror. Sometimes I felt like my hands had caked mud all over the mirror and it couldn't be grimier. But there's not a marriage in past, present, or future history in which either party can say "I have no regrets... I did everything with utmost excellence." There's not a person alive who can say "I am, and have always been, the image of what it looks like to love and cherish another sinner." We all have faults, failures, and regrets. I certainly did. But that's where grace, forgiveness, and perseverance step up to the plate.

I also knew we had told each other that we would give the other person the rest of our lifetime to work things out -- to be transformed. The reality is that's a *really* hard thing to do, as evidenced by divorce statistics. In the toughest times, I had always pressed into my relationship with Jesus and I frequently heard the same whisper: "My grace is sufficient son, because *my* power is made perfect in *your* weakness". At some point in all marriages, I think you have to honestly reflect and ask yourself, "What did you really think 'worse' or 'poorer' or 'sickness' looked like?" Generally, it looks horrible, broke, and in the hospital.

I cried for a while there in the living room before finally telling her I needed to go for a drive. I got in my car, fighting off tears so I could see the road ahead of me, and managed to get to a Wendy's parking lot about eight miles from our house.

I called David.

I called Lucas.

I sobbed, and sobbed, and sobbed. I could barely talk. I have no idea how long the conversations were. They felt like an eternity. I didn't know really what to tell them other than what had happened. They didn't really know how to respond other than to pray.

I went to each of the couples houses in our small group and talked with them, in summary, but in total honesty about the unfolding of that day. We prayed, we cried, and eventually I went home.

It is what the term *'gut-wrenching'* was created for; I don't think you can begin to understand, and neither can I begin to fully describe, this level of pain and hurt unless you've had to go through it or something unfortunately similar.

3

'OBEDIENCE'

Sunday, August 5, 2012

The next morning I got up, as I usually did on Sunday and went to church, arriving about fifteen minutes before the start of the first service. For about two years, I had been volunteering during the first service with the 'snails'. That's what our church calls the six-to-twelve month old crowd. I love working with them because they make me smile every single Sunday -- when they aren't freaking out because they just watched Mommy leave and "Oh wait -- stranger danger! He looks like I should yell at him". But I've earned my honorary PhD as a master distracter over the time back there; I genuinely love my 'snails'; who can be equally as slimy as the real thing.

But they are also the future of the church; it's not so much watching kids for me as it is beginning the investment into the next generation of church leaders. Maybe I'm overly ambitious, but I love praying for them because every now and then, one of them will look at me like they actually understand what I'm saying when I pray for them. I figure Satan doesn't wait until they're at the mystical "age of accountability" to begin working on these kids; why should I let him have first dibs at their lives?

My neighbor across the street had come up to me as I was mowing the grass on Wednesday earlier that week. Whenever that happens, I am somewhat afraid that I unknowingly slung a rock into their window with my lawn mower. Fortunately, he was just coming to tell me that Mark Rutland (current President of Orel Roberts University, Global

Servants, and The Herald of Joy), one of my top five favorite pastors/ speakers ever, was going to be at another church in our town that Sunday. I had decided I would skip the second service at our church and go over to this other church (religious people should 'gasp' at this point) to hear Dr. Rutland speak. And so I left and figured I would arrive only about fifteen minutes or so late.

On my drive over, I remembered the week before that I had fasted while my wife was out of town on a business trip. I can't really explain it; I just felt God calling me very clearly to fast for our marriage.

I'd never fasted for more than two consecutive days before, so a seven-day fast was honestly a bit unfathomable. But my marriage was a bigger deal and I had no idea what else to do to try and make a dent in anything. So I fasted.

Each day, I recalled, through things I would read in the Bible, through worship songs I would listen to, through my time fixed on God in prayer… I kept having the same word, the same theme, the same phrase standout every day.

Obedience.

The last day of the fast, I was 'scrunch-praying'; the kind of praying you do when you're trying to infiltrate the mind of God and scrunching your eyebrows to somehow try and see through the crack in the curtain at what He's doing. I felt like, of all things, God was making it very clear to me, "Son, all I want from you right now is to be obedient". I didn't know what to read that day in my 'quiet time', so I just flipped open to something in the Old Testament I hadn't read in a while, the Book of Nahum.

I stopped at the seventh verse of the first chapter, which simply reads, *"The Lord is good, a refuge in times of trouble. He cares for those who trust in Him"* (NIV).

I simply told God that I believed He is [good & a refuge], and that He does [care for those who trust in Him] -- even if the answer to my prayers doesn't take shape like I hoped and prayed it would.

That said, I don't know if you've ever been on a seven day fast, but to prove to you I'm not more spiritual or holier-than-thou, I was honestly thinking "aaaand?… a little more than 'be obedient' would be nice God

-- I've been without anything but water and some juice for seven days." But that was all He gave me, which is always enough.

On my drive over, I also remembered the page and a half letter I had written to Dr. Rutland back on April 17th, approximately 4 ½ months beforehand. I had felt this nagging for some reason to write to him in February. I put it off and put it off until finally I was like "oh what the heck, might as well write the letter".

It was a rather general letter outlining some of the main struggles in our marriage. In the last paragraph of the letter, I wrote these words,

> "…I'm not entirely sure why I felt inclined to write to you having never met you, but if you have anything that the Holy Spirit might speak to you or through you, I would greatly appreciate it."

I had been listening to him on one of the local radio stations for several years during my lunch breaks and just something in my spirit connected with this man. So I sent the letter off and figured I might hear something back from him in 2013… maybe.

I arrived at the other church (gasp), walked over the river and through the woods from the back parking lot of the church, got a seat between two complete strangers, and figured the band was closing out the worship set, having arrived late as planned.

The senior pastor was out of town that weekend (thus Dr. Rutland being at the church), so the pastor's mother got up on stage and began to give a brief introduction for Dr. Rutland. I remember her saying "Dr. Rutland has such an encouraging word for us today on 'hope' and I just know you're going to be blessed by it." She went on to close out the introduction and welcome him on stage.

As Dr. Rutland took the microphone, he said something like this: "You know, I plan my chapel messages for ORU about a year in advance; it's just how I do it. But as we were standing here worshiping during the last song, the Holy Spirit spoke to me and said I was not to speak on 'hope' as I did in the first service."

"Now, I've been doing this for decades and you'd think I'd learn by now that God does not look down on my sermon calendar and say 'Oh, is that what we're going to speak on that day big-boy!?' He has told me the message for this service is *not* going to be about 'hope'."

I sat there in my own little world -- the only way I know how to describe it is, it's the clear, still, manifest voice of the Holy Spirit in the life of an ordinary Believer.

I distinctly heard the whisper "He's going to talk about obedience".

I sat there dumbfounded and my head began to shake itself. I whispered under my breath, "No way... no... frickin'... way".

Dr. Rutland continued, "You know, in a church like this, whenever there is a guest speaker, everyone gets all excited. Everyone expects this biiiiiggggg revelation, this biiiigggg word from God; [laughing] today is not that day. The message for this service is foundational, fundamental, basic, Christianity 101. Today, for this service, the word I believe the Lord has told me to preach on... is 'obedience'."

I don't know how to accurately describe what I felt, but it was like plunging into a Chattahoochee River in the heat and humidity of a Georgia summer; whole-body refreshment in an instant.

I shook my head in absolute disbelief at what my ears had just heard. I think I literally laughed out loud.

And I wrote Dr. Rutland a letter that week, attaching the initial letter to this second one. In synopsis, this is what it said:

Dear Dr. Rutland,
    I wrote you the attached letter back in April. I hadn't figured I would get a response anytime quickly, so when I found out you were coming to [church name] in town, I had to come. Things in our marriage had continued to go downhill from when I wrote in April, to the point that my wife told both me and our counselors on Saturday, August 4th, that she was done with our marriage and she just wanted out. You came to speak Sunday, August 5th.
    I had fasted the week of July 21 - 28, simply asking God what He wanted from me. Each day, through various places in the Word, music I was listening to, and my prayer time, I just felt like God was simply telling me to be obedient; that obedience was all He wants from me. Frankly, I was expecting something a little 'bigger' than that after seven days, but the more I thought about

it, I realized that is a huge truth. Then you show up a week later, having not responded to my letter, and preached "The Miracle In The Dessert" passage from Acts about foundational obedience to God.

I am convinced of this: When I walked into the sanctuary, in His providence and unique power, God spoke to you to change your planned sermon because He knew I was there. The voice of the Holy Spirit that beckoned me for several months to write you in the first place because, quoting my own words in April "I'm not entirely sure why I felt inclined to write to you having never met you, but if you have anything that the Holy Spirit might speak to you or through you, I would greatly appreciate it." And speak He did.

I find myself, with divorce potentially staring me in the face, so many tears already shed, and having no idea what the future now looks like, laughing in my inner man at the goodness of God. I simply shake my head and think 'Who am I, that the Almighty God would bring the one person in the United States I had written to... from Tulsa, Oklahoma to Gainesville, Georgia... the very weekend this is all going down... change his message between the two services... and confirm the *one word* He had spoken to me throughout the fast the week before... which I had requested from you nearly 4 months before? Truly, where can I go from Your Presence Lord?" Not a whole lot else to say... thank you for your ministry, your testimony, and most especially, your obedience. Right foot, left foot,

4

FOR WHOM THE
LITTLE BELL TOLLS

Monday, August 13, 2012

The following Monday, I'm having my 'quiet time' with God in the morning, sitting in my old brown recliner as usual. I got this chair for free; it's older than I am I think. The recliner is the stereotypical old chair; it's not that ugly or anything heinous like that, it's just soooo comfortable you can't think to ever part with it. It's like your favorite pair of underwear -- you know one day it's going to have to go, but today is not that day!

I begin cycling through my scripture memory verses for that day of the week. Again, so I don't appear more 'learned' or 'spiritual' than I am, the average 5th grader would have committed these to memory in about half the time I do; I just have a horrible memory so it takes an extra degree of discipline on my part unfortunately. I keep my memory verses in an old-school 3x5in index card holder; it's vintage green like the Tupperware in the '70's. Represent.

Doodle is working on her memory verse
as well… "Thou shalt not mooch".

I came to one of the index cards that had a verse which I love and had memorized 4-5 years ago. I had kind of forgotten parts of the verse so I was re-learning it; again, retention... not my strong suit.

But I flipped over this card, began reading/quoting the passage,

"2 Chronicles 20:17... 'You will not have to fight this battle,' declares the Lord. 'Go, take up your positions, stand firm, and see the deliverance the Lord will give you, Judah and Jerusalem. Do not be discouraged, do not be dismayed. Go out to face them tomorrow and the Lord will be with you". (NIV)

As I finished reading it -- again, the only way I know how to describe it is in Holy Spirit acoustics -- I distinctly perceived this little bell (yes, odd I know, but it was like a little hotel bellhop 'bing-bing' bell sound) had been wrung on the right side of the index card, which preceded this message from the Holy Spirit: "Jacob, this is not your battle. You have a position to take in prayer, you have a place to stand, but this is not your fight son."

And that was it.

I felt oddly encouraged, but said nothing to anyone. I mean, what do you really say?

5

THE BATTLE I DIDN'T FIGHT

Wednesday, August 22, 2012

The following week I had a real estate finance class from Monday through Friday. I was already signed up for it and could not opt out without losing the fees, which were substantial.

Note to the world: math is normally horrible; when you're going through the second week of your marriage imploding, it is downright satanic.

The course for the week was effectively a college finance class compressed into one week amidst the most emotionally challenging period of my life to date.

These are the things that cause people to drink.

On the second or third day of the week, the course facilitator -- we'll call her Debbie -- was up in front of our class of fifteen or so giving her normal 'housekeeping & agenda-de-jour' announcements. She is an incredible ambassador, not only of the company and organization she represents in her professional career, but also of life in general. I don't know if I've ever met another human being with more genuine zeal for life... at 8:00am sharp. I joked with her one day about "random" drug testing. She told me a former employer had actually had her tested because they literally thought she was "on something". She makes the Energizer Bunny look like he's sleep-walking with lead slippers.

Anyway, she gets done her normal spiel and then says something like this, "Hey guys, people sometimes ask me why I do what I do. I do this because I love... absolutely love what I do [insert jazz hands]! I wake up every day and can't wait to come to work. And if this isn't what you love doing -- then go do what you love. This isn't for everyone, but everyone has something that they love doing, so if this isn't it, then find whatever it is and go do it."

I found myself having an internal re-hash of a conversation there in the classroom, which I've had over and over with myself.

"You're good at what you are doing, but you spend all your free time and mental energy thinking of something else -- the *same something else*. You've been told several times by different people when asking them about going into full-time ministry 'how do you know?', to which there has been the same response: 'when you can do nothing else'. It's not that you can do nothing else; You've been good at quite a few things in your professional life. But you are consumed with one thing -- the same one thing: feeding sheep."

So I had gotten a hotel room for the week, since it ended up being cheaper for my boss to put me up in a hotel than pay mileage for the whole week. A good friend and mentor of mine, Donnie, happened to live just outside Marietta, GA where the classes were being held. So Donnie and I scheduled dinner on Wednesday night of that week. We agreed to meet up at a local barbeque restaurant; because when math and marriage converge, you need major doses of pork, sweet tea, and old waitresses calling you "Sugar Pie" to offset the pain.

It just makes sense people.

We talked about a lot of things. Marriage, ministry stuff, life stuff, job stuff -- we probably spent two hours in the restaurant just talking through things. Around the two hour mark is, when I'm led to believe, they actually change the sweet tea out with Turbo-Lax to let you know you've worn out your welcome. So we retreated down the street to the only place you go in The South after having a hearty pork-on-pork meal -- Krispy Kreme Doughnuts.

Don't judge me.

We finally left there, prayed, and parted; him back to his house and family, me back to my hotel room to figure out what parts of the room were cleaned and what parts were given the old "that looks clean enough" once over.

The next day, Donnie sent me an email. I don't remember exactly what it said, but I remember reading it in my hotel room and, like in church, involuntarily shaking my head and literally laughing out loud as I read it.

His email read something like this... "Jake, thanks for sharing and talking through things last night. I am encouraged by your faith through all of this and as I was praying about your situation this morning, I felt like the Holy Spirit was prodding me to tell you to read 2 Chronicles 20 and to know that it is the Lord who fights the battle for us."

As I leaned forward on the hotel chair to make sure I had actually just read what I thought I'd just read, I shook my head and laughed, saying to myself, "Of all the chapters in all of the books in all The Bible -- the very same one God?! You told *him* the very same one You told *me* last week! You are un-believable... Thank You!"

6

PREPARING OF THE
HEART BEGINS

Summary from Journal Entry: Tuesday, September 25, 2012

God, I have no earthly idea what You are up to.

Having begun reading Katie Davis' book, "Kisses From Katie" I am speechless. The heart of this person, the heart of selfless obedience -- Even as I write this, I can picture what my face looks like -- just utter dismay, amazement, and a bit of "what is about to happen?"

I picked up this book on Amazon.com with the book about Ravi and the other one about South Africa; I don't even remember where I heard about this, but I am enraptured. I cried over the Introduction -- who the heck cries over the intro to a book they can't remember how they came across?!

Last night, I read a chapter... and cried. This morning, another chapter... and cried. What... the... heck... is... happening?!

Father, the longing of my heart for over nine years has been the cry to make a difference in the Kingdom that would leave a mark for You.

I have absolutely no idea what I am doing; I can't even believe I am writing this. Find my life when I lose it for Your sake, huh? Not until I lose it will I find it. Holy Spirit, please remind me constantly, that You do not operate on human logic.

I am captivated by this person; this courageous servant who is the face of obedience if there ever was one. Jesus, whatever You want, whenever You say so, whatever the direction may be, I want my life to have this kind of impact. Keep me from being stupid, but Father, don't let me think I'm being so wise I become disobedient. Take this life and make it Yours. Last request… a little confirmation would be nice because You know how slow I can be.

7

FOUR SIMPLE WORDS

Thursday, September 27, 2012

Tonight I went out to walk and spend some alone time praying.

It was a beautiful night... about 70 degrees and crisp Fall air setting
in. Nightfall had come and as I was strolling down the faded asphalt
street, some sort of critter was "playing chicken" with me in the middle
of the street. It was coming towards me in the road -- I couldn't make
out what kind of animal it was. It could have been a cat, opossum or
raccoon, but it also could have been a skunk.

Better safe than sorry.

So I conceded and turned around. This cut down my time walking,
so I found a place to sit and pray next to the little Baptist church that
is on the way to the park where I had intended to walk. I had selected
a big oak tree as my back rest. Leaning over, I used my hand to brush
away the few loose rocks and acorns that were at its base. I turned myself
around and plopped down, sitting 'Indian-style' against the tree and
just stared across the parking lot into nothing but a wall of trees being
illuminated by the dull orange glow of the street light nearby.

Over the course of the hour or so that I sat there praying and
thinking about all that was going on, I found myself overwhelmed at
both what was going on in my 'here & now' life, but also in what I felt
like God was starting to make very clear that He wanted as part of my
future.

I was asking God for confirmation -- ABUNDANT confirmation that this calling is Him and not me. I found myself at one point with tears in my eyes, asking God out loud, "Why me, God? Why on earth would You choose me?"

I asked this same question, out loud, three times. After the third time, the same voice -- the same soft whisper that spoke to me "obedience" during the fast and 2 Chronicles 20 -- whispered four simple words:

"Because you will go."

8

THE BUSINESS CARD

Journal Entry: Friday, September 28, 2012

Met Prudential guy at Steve & Robby's new property. His business card has a quote at the bottom of it: "The best way to make a difference with your life is to make a difference in someone else's". [He's a freakin' realtor?!] What on earth is happening? God, I realize I should probably "get it" by now, given the onslaught of things this week, but I am still just a bit bewildered.

God, provided we get past November, and Your confirmation continues as it has been this week, the house will go up for sale and this whole process will start. I know the feeling Katie was talking about this morning where your heart feels like it's going to explode within you -- I had it this afternoon on my drive home. No more gnawing cry from my heart about a meaningful life for the Kingdom; instead, today a feeling like if I wasn't wearing a shirt, I would be able to see the shape of my heart protruding from my chest.

I am reminded tonight, as I get in bed to read another chapter, of the movie "End Of The Spear". I'm not really sure where that came to mind as I haven't watched it in years, but I remember the grip on my heart and the tears I cried at the end of the movie. I remember being asked why I was crying -- and I remember sniveling out "Because I want my life to matter like that for God. I want to have an impact like that."

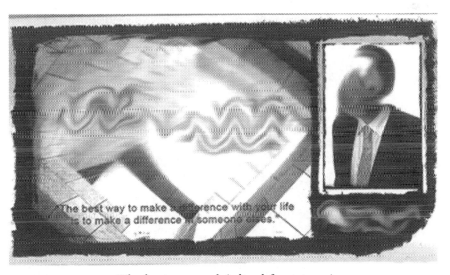

The business card (edited for privacy)

9

MY MEMORY KEITH

Tuesday, October 9, 2012

Over the last month, for a reason I could not explain, I felt like God was putting two particular scripture passages on the forefront of my heart for me to memorize. I don't know how else to describe it other than it was like He was trying to drive these into my heart like you press a clove of garlic through a garlic press -- getting all up in 'my bidness'.

Let me preface this with saying that when I surrendered my life to Christ on March 23, 2003 at 9:02am in a dirt parking lot just outside of Clemson, SC, there were a lot of changes in my life that ensued.

One of the more 'spiritual' changes, which has, thankfully, stayed with me through present day, was/is memorizing and meditating on passages in The Bible. I owe that to The Navigators at Clemson University and my buddy Lucas.

Because thoughts lead to beliefs and beliefs lead to actions, scripture memory is an effective way of renewing my mind -- and mine needs constant correcting. We all, or at least most of us, want to do the right thing. Jesus is the best example of someone who always did the right thing (if you don't think so, I guarantee it's because you've never read the four Gospels. You might be surprised at what you find out about Jesus). So if I want to be like Him, I need to think like Him, which means I need to get His words in between my ears.

Honestly, sometimes I think I'm something special for doing it; until, that is, I remember that in the Jewish culture when The Bible was written, people – children -- were memorizing entire books of the

Old Testament -- or possibly the entire thing. Aaaand, I come back to humble planet Earth and realize if I were in that culture, I'd probably be riding the short bus (or miniature donkey) to school.

These two scripture passages were just... just odd to me. They had a central theme which, as I look back through all the passages and verses I have memorized and review each week, I realized I had NEVER memorized anything on this one topic.

Generosity.

Nine years... not one single verse on generosity. Virtually every other Biblical topic I had memorized numerous passages on: life, joy, sin, salvation, forgiveness, death, temptation, endurance, hope, guidance, evangelism, serving others, trusting God -- you name it, there was at least one; yet not a single one on generosity

Perplexing.

These are/were the two passages... Psalm 112:4-5 & 2 Corinthians 9:6-11

Ps 112:4-5 – "Even in darkness light dawns for the upright, for those who are gracious and compassionate and righteous. ⁵ Good will come to him who is generous and lends freely, who conducts his affairs with justice." (NIV)

2 Cor 9:6-11 – "Remember this: Whoever sows sparingly will also reap sparingly, and whoever sows generously will also reap generously. ⁷ Each of you should give what you have decided in your heart to give, not reluctantly or under compulsion, for God loves a cheerful giver. ⁸ And God is able to make all grace abound, so that in all things at all times, having all that you need, you will abound in every good work. ⁹ As it is written: 'He has scattered abroad His gifts to the poor; His righteousness endures forever.' ¹⁰ Now He who supplies seed to the sower and bread for food will also supply and increase your store of seed and will increase the harvest of your righteousness. ¹¹ You will be made rich in every way so that you can be generous on every occasion, and through us your generosity will result in thanksgiving to God." (NIV)

Again, to put my 'spirituality' in context here, I memorized the first passage fairly quickly because it was short and succinct. The second passage -- frankly, I kind of fought with God over it for about two weeks -- because I was just being flat out lazy. I was like "Uh, God, yeah -- You know how that passage is five verses long... yeah... I was thinking maybe we could do one that was like one or two verses long, You know, that still packs the same punch and everything -- for Jesus, that is". That travelled about as far as a submarine with a doggy-door at both ends.

So one Saturday at the end of September, I had gone out for a hike; just me, my Camelbak, my Bible, Katie's book, my journal, and about a million thoughts running through my head.

A short rabbit trail here, but I saw a black bear at around twenty-to-thirty yards away on my hike. I was just walking along on the gravel forest service road, when it walked out of the woods, stopped and turned to stare directly at me for about four or five seconds, and then ran off into the woods.

It was one of those moments in life when all of a sudden, you find yourself saying "Uhhh... Bear... Bear... it's a bear... it's a live bear... (bear runs away)... I... saw... a... bear!!" I really wanted to have someone else there at that moment to do an end-zone touchdown high-five or chest bump. It was awesome... after I didn't become a victim of a bear attack. Next time I need to bring my buffalo (YouTube... Guy on a buffalo... do yourself a favor).

So literally I had spent the majority of the 2hrs hiking out praying, venting, throwing my hands up -- you name it, to God. I stopped for about thirty minutes to read the chapter in Katie's book entitled "Amazing Grace", about one of Katie's girls, Grace, which I'll never forget. There was a beautiful little purple and yellow wildflower next to where I was sitting, so I picked it, fastened it in my Camelbak, and thought, "You never know. You might get to give this to Grace one day?"

13

AMAZING GRACE

The Purple Flower

I loaded up my stuff to begin the 2hr hike back and, as I started moving, I felt my 'verse pack' (what I call the little pouch I keep my scripture memory cards in -- about the size of a business card holder) in my right front pocket of my shorts.

And it was like in an instant, God spoke to me and said, "Hey you! You know how you've spent the last two hours talking and praying and jibber-jabbering? How about you spend the next two getting this in your head and chewing on it for a while?"

I say this with some degree of embarrassment, but I believe my first reaction to this was to roll my eyes and give a resigning sigh; the kind you do when your parents have finally worn you down on cleaning your room when you were a kid.

I spent the next two hours repeating and trying to memorize those five verses. I only got three down. See, I told you I would have ridden the miniature donkey back in the day! Through the course of the next week, I FINALLY got the full five verses down pat. That was Sunday, October 7th.

Two days later, Tuesday, October 9th, was like any other day at my office. Doing bills, work orders, visiting a property or two -- the run-of-the-mill morning. For lunch that day I had the "brown-bag-special", so I took my food and the book I happened to be reading at the time, "Walking from East to West" (an autobiography of Ravi Zacharias) into our conference room, and, as you might guess: ate and read (uh-der).

I noted one thing while I was reading. It was during part of Ravi's description of why, at one point in his adolescence, he had tried to take his own life. In essence, he described it like this: People who turn to that path as the course of their death do so because they have tried to fill the "why" in their lives with the "what" -- the job, the house, the bank account, the relationship, the you name it -- the temporal things which do not and will not satisfy the eternal thing we were created for; to know our Creator.

I went back to my desk and sat down on my gray ergo-ball-chair, which I had gotten a week prior to help with my horrendous posture (it's probably one of the better 'health' investments I've made to be honest). I'm sitting there, trying to look like I'm working and not having too much fun on my personal bouncy-castle, when in walks my assistant, Shelly (who had been out showing a property), and some guy I didn't recognize.

Shelly just looked at me and said, "Jake, he [signaling to the man] would like to speak to you" and went on into her office. So I stood up, thinking this guy was the person she had just been showing the property to, and asked which property this was about.

He responded, "No -- no, it's not like that." So then I thought to myself, "Hmm, maybe he's one of the many tenants I've never met before?" So I asked him "I'm sorry, which property are you at?" He responded the same way as the first question.

So at this point, me feeling a little awkward, I have him come into my office from the foyer of our front waiting area and tell him to have a seat.

I ask him his name, which he tells me, is "Keith".

"What can I do for you Keith?" I ask.

As he began speaking, I started to look at his face and could tell he was either on something or he'd been crying in the not too distant past. He effectively told me that he had spent the last two nights (in the 40's those two nights) sleeping at the back of an asphalt parking lot. He proceeded to explain that he had been kicked out of his apartment, saying his landlord/super had taken his rent money and not given it to the owner; he had no paperwork to prove otherwise, and now had been evicted (I didn't get into all the details because I really didn't care to).

He explained that he had a job and showed me his badge, along with his driver's license to verify he was who he said he was. He told me he worked 2nd shift and had to be at work in a couple hours. [In case you're wondering, this has never happened to me before -- ever, at any job I've ever had. No one has ever come into my place of work before asking for help or something like this.]

He continued talking.

I eventually stopped him.

"Keith, what do you need man?" I asked, looking straight at him.

He struggled and stammered a bit to come out with it, but eventually said he had found a place he could sleep for the rest of the week and just needed thirty-five dollars to pay for this accommodation until he got paid that Friday.

He continued to talk, but it was like the Holy Spirit vacuumed my consciousness out of the room and brought those two passages onto display in the theater of my mind... *"You will be made rich in every way so that you can be generous on every occasion and your generosity to us will result in thanksgiving to God"*... *"Good will come to him who is generous and lends freely"*.

He was still talking.

I interrupted him.

"Keith," I asked, "what time do you have to be at work?"

"3:15pm" he responded.

I glanced at my watch... 12:45pm.

"Come on -- let's go for a ride," I said.

We went out of my office, past the front foyer, down the stairs, and into my car without a word to anyone. We hopped into my car and I said this:

"Keith, I have no idea why God does what He does nor do I understand the way He does it, but you had an appointment today with Jesus Christ. We're going to do better than $35. We're going to go get you some clothes, whatever toiletries and supplies you need, I'm guessing you haven't eaten lunch, so we'll get some food, and then we'll do the thirty-five dollars, and get you to work on time."

There's something very refreshing about seeing a grown man weep -- no gimmicks, no mask, no hiding behind their own 'goodness' or 'achievement' -- just total overwhelmed brokenness being met with a measure of God's grace I don't know that I fully understand just yet.

I took him first to Marshall's to get some clothes. As we were walking in the store, he just kept saying, "I can't believe this is happening -- I just can't believe it -- this is like something you see on TV, but this never happens in real life!"

I gave him carte blanche.

"I don't know what you need man," I stated, "but if you need it, get it".

As I was waiting on him to pick things out, I heard that little voice of Satan whispering, "This dude's going to take you for a ride sucker! Just wait and see what the cash register pings up."

Keith came back, thirty minutes later, with... one shirt, one pair of pants, and one jacket. I could see he had this look of hesitation on his face and looked down the far aisle. "What is it? Is there something else?" I asked. He said there was also a pair of boots he could use (since he had a job on his feet eight hours per day with no car or bike to get to work), but they were kind of expensive and he already felt so overwhelmed. So he tried them on, I bent down and checked where his big toe was (still can't believe I did that), and we grabbed them with the other things and went to check out. We then went to Publix to get some toiletries and then to Burger King, which was the closest fast food restaurant to his job and where he was staying the rest of the week.

I got him a gift card so he could eat the rest of the week and sat down with him in one of the corner booths. We had been talking intermittently between the car and the stores over the course of an hour, but spent the next hour at BK talking face-to-face.

"Keith," I told him, "let me be very clear with you; this, all of this, is not about me being a nice or generous person -- (I shared with him those two passages God had laid on my heart over the past month). This is about Jesus Christ confirming His voice in my life and making an inarguable demonstration of His love and grace in your life today. This is a small -- tiny, tiny, tiny picture of the grace that Jesus invites us into as His sons and daughters."

I continued, "You literally could have walked into hundreds -- HUNDREDS of different offices today, but God brought you into the one office, to the one person, whose heart He had laid this timely word on over the last month -- knowing that you would walk into my office today and be the embodiment and opportunity for me to live it out... *and* knowing exactly what you needed, when you felt all hope was lost. He knew you needed to hear from Him; to know that He still loves you with all His heart."

At one point Keith said he wondered what life was like as "one of those people I see passing me on the sidewalk" -- someone walking a dog, or pushing kids in a stroller, or dressed in a suit talking on their cell phone. "If I could just be there," he said, "I think I'd really be happy -- I'd really have something."

I responded with the very sentiment from Ravi's book and then shared with him the summary of a *60 Minutes* interview I had watched recently on YouTube with Tom Brady, the Quarterback for the New England Patriots.

Here's a guy who literally has everything a man could ever want: millions of dollars, a literal supermodel on his arm, endless endorsements, is a future Hall of Famer, has arguably the best job in the country on one of the best franchises in the history of professional football -- and is frankly -- a stud.

Yet in the interview, he expresses emptiness. "There's gotta be more than this" I believe are his exact words in response to the interviewers question, "So what else is there for Tom Brady?"

I said, "Keith, this is a guy, who, literally, has every 'what' in the world at his disposal -- fame, money, women, success -- whatever he wants, he can have it. Yet he is EMPTY -- he says he's EMPTY -- because all these things are the 'what' that will never fill the 'why'. And all these things you see on the sidewalk, they are just more of the 'what' that will *never satisfy* the 'why' inside you or I."

As we wrapped up our time together and I brought him back to where he was staying, he said something I'll never forget for the rest of my life.

"Honestly," Keith said, "I was just thankful that you took the time to listen to me. That was all I really wanted -- all I needed -- just to have someone care and not slam a door in my face. All this other stuff, I mean -- I could have never -- would have never, asked for all this or thought this was ever possible."

I laughed a little to myself, looked him straight in the eyes.

"Keith," I said, with some degree of disbelief, "man -- that's the Gospel! All Jesus wants from us is to come to Him, in our brokenness, our sinfulness [note to the world: Jesus didn't allow Himself to get murdered for 'mistakers'], and in just plain humility and share our soul's emptiness in absolute candor -- just to have our Creator listen -- just *that*

-- that He would even take the time to listen -- It's *amazing*! But His problem is this: He loves us. He *really* loves us -- because He *is* Love. And because of that, He cannot stop with an attentive ear. He gives us immeasurably, abundantly beyond all we could ever ask or think possible -- beyond our wildest imaginations. We're invited, welcomed, in to His Kingdom and all that is His becomes ours. That... is... the Gospel."

I concluded, "But there's good news and bad news that comes with this: The good news is, Jesus Christ wants you to know, beyond a shadow of a doubt, that He still has a plan and purpose for your life. He knew exactly where you were today and by your own admission, that is undeniable. The bad news is, since you know that, you can never be the same again."

[as a follow up note from a couple people who have asked "Did you ever see Keith again?" the answer is a grinning "YES!!". He stopped by my office in February and looked like a completely different person. He said he had shared what had happened in his life with several people he worked with that were down-and-out and needed the encouragement. Sounded a little to me like 'Go, therefore and make disciples' to me.]

10

THE ABC'S FROM GOD

Journal Entry: Wednesday, October 10, *2012*

Ridiculous.

First journal entry from my office... ever. Got caught up on some stuff at work and decided for some reason to open up the Atlanta Business Chronicle instead of chunking it in the trash like I normally do. [The whole time I'm handling and opening the paper, my hands seem to be operating independent from my brain -- literally, as my hands begin to reach for the paper on top of my filing cabinet and open it, I have this expression on my face that signifies the sentiment of my brain -- "What... are... you... doing? Why on earth are you opening this? You seriously would be more interested in a chemistry paper on the composition of dirt. What are you opening this paper for? Google something -- Google the word 'something' for heaven's sake -- this is the Atlanta... Business... Chronicle?!"]

Opened up the International section for whatever reason [if I could care less about the ABC, I reeeeally could care less about the International section] and unfolded the first page. I saw a familiar face; it was a picture of Georgia's Senator Isakson... giving some food... to some black kids... in Uganda. Whaaaaat?! I'm sitting here absolutely bah-lown away. Of all people, of all articles that could have been done, of all places Isakson could have (or has) gone... the only ABC I have *ever* opened... and the one place that has been on my mind every day the last month or so. Just flabbergasted God, just absolutely dumbfounded.

11

THE DELIVERY

Wednesday, October 24, 2012

It's around 9:00pm on Thursday night, October 11th, and my mom calls.

It may not be odd to you, but my mom never calls that late, so I pick up the phone half-expecting to hear that something is wrong, someone's gravely ill, hospitalized, the dog died -- a Russian tank is in the front yard -- who knows? This is how the conversation goes:

Mom: "Hey sweetie, I had a weird phone call today. You remember Mr. Jameson, the neighbor from our old house?"

Me: "Yeah"

Mom: "He called today and said there was a package delivered to the old house for you. The person who lives there now asked him if he knew who a 'Jacob Moran' was. Of course, he said it was one of the sons of the person who used to live there. The package is from Barnes & Nobles… did you order anything from there? Or do you know anyone who would have sent you something at the old address?"

Me: "Uhh… nope"

Mom: "Well, what do you want me to tell him?"

> Me: "Hmm... well... I guess if you can get it from him, just forward it on to me."

Now for a little context.

Six years ago, my mom got re-married. She had been at this house, next to the Jameson's, for several years, but had moved in to her now husband's house once they got married.

I, however, had only lived in the house next to the Jameson's for about four months... eight years ago.

So when she called me, I went through a quick mental list of questions:

> Did I order anything from Amazon?
> It's not my birthday right?
> Am I expecting anything from anyone?
> Could it be a mail bomb?"

> Nope, nope, nope, and... hmm.
> Then I had this very weird thought/sensation.
> "Whaaaat are You up to God?"

I waited almost two weeks until the forwarded package arrived in the mail at my office the morning of Wednesday, October 24th. I opened the package in front of my laptop -- and started laughing.

From some address in Illinois, completely foreign and unknown to me, someone had mailed to me (not Current Resident), Perry Noble's "Unleash!". To some reading this, that may not mean a whole lot. To me, it was God thumping me on the forehead, as if to say "Hello McFly... can you hear Me now???"

Perry is the pastor of NewSpring Church in Anderson, SC -- the very church I was attending when I surrendered my life to Christ in 2003. The church is huge now, but at that time, it was a small-to-medium sized community church that was meeting at Anderson College's auditorium, because they didn't have an actual church building at that point. God has grown their ministry over the past decade to where they now have a bunch of campuses and over twenty thousand in weekly attendance across the state of South Carolina. Understand... the book didn't come from NewSpring. Not only that, but I only attended there for about four months, was never on any membership/mailing list, and had never received anything from their church in the mail -- ever.

As I turned over the back of the book, the book's summary blazed off the back cover. "When you're ready for something truly extraordinary, consider living life Unleashed! Jesus promised us a full and abundant life. But if we're honest, most of us feel as if we're missing out."

I sat back on my bouncy-castle and just shook my head and laughed. About two or three months after I gave my life to Christ, I felt like God put a calling, a beckoning on my life, to be engaged in full-time ministry -- a call that for over 9+ years has only grown. I've just never felt a true soundness with what that looked like for me. But this was as though God was saying, "Remember where this all started. Remember where and when this all began. Remember when the calling came. You've been missing out and you know it, but no longer. You know what I'm telling you to do, now go do it".

That morning I Googled the address it came from. Some single family home in Machesney Park, IL. I had no earthly idea who this book came from, so I scribbled a quick note to the effect of "Hey... know how you ordered this book and mailed it to me... uhh, care to explain?" and sent it off to Illinois, wondering if I'd get a response... or if I'd get a letter back saying "Hey crack-head... I have no idea what you're talking about... Daaa Bears!" I had to at least attempt to get an answer. [fyi... never got a response]

As I began reading Chapter 1 of "Unleash" in the week following, I had no doubt this book was post-marked at a pearly gate. The frequency, the level, the depth, the clarity to which God was making His voice to me was so abundant; all of this, synced with this book, was like God using the precision an astronaut uses to dock a 30 billion dollar piece of equipment into the International Space Station; God was making it virtually impossible for me to miss what He was saying.

Perry writes, "Once we see who He is, we will find it far easier to surrender to what He says -- As we see Him more clearly, we will trust Him more fully -- We will follow Him more intentionally. God is not after our begrudging submission. He is after our joy."

Yes… for whatever reason…
I actually kept the packing slip?! This is it.

12

CONTACT

Thursday, October 25, 2012

I had lunch scheduled with Scott; a friend for years and a true brother-from-another-mother. He and I were set to meet at a local restaurant, Avocado's, on The Square in downtown Gainesville, which is about two blocks from my office. It was an absolutely beautiful Fall day, so I was more than happy to walk to lunch.

We sat down at a table outside on the sidewalk area and, over the hour-long lunch, I shared with Scott a good bit of what I have written about thus far. Having just received *Unleash* the day before, I brought that up at the end of our conversation.

Scott looked at me and said, "Have you talked to Cliff?"

Cliff, at that time, was the High School Pastor at our church, where Scott is also on staff. He also happened to live in my neighborhood and is a fellow Clemson University Alumni... so he's basically awesome.

"Uhh, nope -- about what?" I questioned, as if I was somehow supposed to know what Scott was referring to.

"Cliff just announced that he is leaving at the end of November to go work at NewSpring. You should talk to him about this," he replied.

"Reeaaallllly?! Huh" I answered with a bit of a wrinkle in my brow.

We finished up lunch, prayed, and left.

13

THE FRIEND-OF-
A-FRIEND

Monday, November 12, 2012

I saw Cliff at church, the Wednesday after my lunch with Scott, during PumpkinFest. PumpkinFest is a cracked-out family extravaganza our church puts on for anyone in the local community who wants to come get their kids all hopped up on sugar and then see how high they can bounce on any number of inflatables. It's an event that is awesome to volunteer at because you get to see some really creative costumes, yet you also can't help but feel like your childhood experience got *really* jipped! These kids get four times the amount of candy I used to gather and in half the time, plus they just walk around in a big circle to get it -- not hike up and down hills in three different subdivisions while freezing thy bum off. Such is life.

My favorite picture from PumpkinFest... neither
vintage Batman nor Ironman could stand upright
long enough to swing the pylon.

Cliff and I scheduled lunch for Monday the 12th at another local restaurant just off The Square called The Turnstile Deli. I don't remember what Cliff ordered because I was so fixated on my cornbread and Brunswick stew, which was a perfect fit for the chilly weather that day.

As we sat down to eat, I walked through pretty much the same story I had shared with Scott. As I got to the end, Cliff got the big smile on his face that typifies him -- everyone who knows Cliff, knows the grin I'm talking about.

"That's an awesome story man," Cliff said. "It's exciting to see what God is going to do with all this. You should talk to Trey."

"From the ManTreat?" I asked.

ManTreat was a youth retreat for high school and middle school guys that I had volunteered at in mid-October. It was a joint retreat, with our church and another church, of which Trey was the Youth Pastor at the other church.

"I know who he is, but don't know-him know him," I followed.

"Trey and his Dad go to Uganda all the time. I don't know all of what they do, but I know they're over there all the time. You should find some time and talk to him about this," Cliff said.

We sat there taking this all in and at one point just couldn't help but started laughing and shaking our heads in the "this is craziness" kind of reaction you have when you are just overwhelmed at what God is doing.

Seriously -- who lives in Gainesville, GA and goes to Uganda "all the time"??

14

THE FACEBOOK POST

Wednesday, November 21, 2012… Day before Thanksgiving.

I had travelled up to Simpsonville, SC to stay a few days with some close friends, Lucas & Christie, and some extended family members of theirs. Thursday morning the kids are up -- playing with about 16 toys at the same time, while sporting footie pajamas and a mean case of 'bed-head'.

I miss being a kid.

I sat down on their red sofa and between the toys and people passing through the living room, attempted to have my quiet time. I only got four verses into the chapter I was reading, which was all I needed that day.

I was reading through John and came to Chapter eleven; commonly referred to as "the Death of Lazarus" chapter. In verse four, Jesus basically tells His audience that even though Lazarus has died, this is not the end of him. His audience has got to be thinking, "Umm… does Jesus know that, uhh… he's been dead -- like dead-dead? Like, the kind of dead where we kind of buried him several days ago". It reminds me, oddly, of the scene in one of the Austin Powers movie's where the Will Ferrell's character drives off the cliff and then, from below says "I… I'm not dead yet… I'm just very badly wounded." Not a great movie, but a very funny scene.

Jesus goes on to say, rather than this happening to cause sorrow, this actually happened so that God would be glorified. When I read accounts like this in The Bible, I often place myself in the story, trying to imagine Jesus saying that and thinking, "Say whaaaat?!"

But as I read this, it was like God translated this account into a reflecting pool that was and is my life. I felt like He was simply saying, "Son, this divorce is not the end of you; rather, I will use even this so that I might be glorified in and through your life." As I imagine Jesus' audience probably thought when they heard His words regarding Lazarus, it was one of those moments where you just have to take a deep sigh, shrug your shoulders, and lean on your faith *in* God rather than your understanding *of* God. His ways are not our ways.

How can He use the death of a close friend to bring glory to Himself? No one understood or could conceive of how that was even possible *until* it actually happened; until he walked out of the tomb. Same goes for me. I have no earthly idea how divorce could ever result in God being glorified, but I know His voice and I know He is faithful.

I sat reflecting on this a few minutes amidst the playing and games going on around me and then picked up my iPhone and pulled up Facebook to see what was going on in the lives of my friends.

Our church's pastor, Dr. Tom (who rarely posts things on Facebook) had posted something a few minutes before. It was the first thing on my screen. A link to an online article -- about Uganda; a country our church does not currently have any ministry outreach in.

I sat there staring at my phone feeling like God was saying, "Will ya lookie there?! Hey, you asked me to make it so obvious even you couldn't miss it, right?"

15

FORTUNE COOKIES

Friday, November 30, 2012

I arrived back at my house after spending a few days with Lucas and Christie and their family. It was my first night back at my house... my partially emptied house that felt entirely broken. I didn't feel like doing much of anything, had nearly an entire kitchen that was now gone, and knew I needed to eat something. So after I unloaded the car, I decided I'd run out to the closest shopping center I could think of for Chinese take-out. I called in the order and hopped in the car, feeling like I was in a bit of a meandering daze going to pick up my brown bag dinner. While I love Chinese food, it has a way of ruining the smell of your car for a good twenty-four hours, so I booked it on the way home.

I think fortune cookies are pretty lame, so if I have the opportunity, I eat them before the meal, so as to break any sort of superstition over the little pieces of paper that come from the industrial plant. Say it ain't so! C'mon, these are made by machines, not leprechauns.

When I got home, I had two fortune cookies in my brown bag. I opened both, threw the cookies in my mouth and held the little crumpled pieces of paper open -- and laughed. I took a picture and texted it to Lucas. His response -- "Wow".

This was my first meal back in an empty house.

This was the picture I texted to Lucas of the original fortune cookie wrappers.

16

THE INITIAL MEETING

Monday, December 3, 2012

I had contacted Trey and, over a few email exchanges, we scheduled lunch at a throwback burger joint called The Collegiate, just off The Square. If I'm nothing else in life, I'm consistent! The Collegiate has about eight things on their menu -- all of which make your face smile with comfort. Once every three or four months, one of the local conference centers hosts Eastman's Gun Show directly across the street. There's really nothing like buying a shotgun and then walking across the street for an old-fashioned cheeseburger with a homespun Cherry Coke.

'murica.

So at this point, I've refined the story of the last few months down to a science. I shared it with Trey. He was, of course, very familiar with Katie Davis and the Amazima ministry she started in Uganda. He shared with me what his father had gotten involved with several years ago over in Uganda; a full-blown ministry effort targeting issues with poverty, disease, ministry training -- pretty much a full-scale project.

Then he said, "So when can you go?"

"Uhh, well I was thinking probably sometime in the early-to-mid summer timeframe. I'm hoping to head down to Honduras in February or March to visit two of the kids I've sponsored down there through Compassion International and then figure out some way to go to Uganda," I replied.

"Can you flip-flop that?" he asked. "I'm taking a group in March. I'd love to have you come with us if you can work that out. The cost difference of the plane ticket between March and June is $1,000, so you might want to consider that in your travel plans," he said.

"March huh? I... I could do that," I said.

We wrapped up our conversation and Trey said he thought the next logical step would be to put me in touch with his Dad, who was the main point person for Uganda and go from there. So on December 10th I got a call from his Dad, Loren, and we went from there.

17

THE LETTER FROM ME

Tuesday, December 11, 2012

While trying to get settled (if there is such a thing) back into a now, partially furnished house, I had begun going through some old boxes… trying to consolidate some things, identify what I wanted to donate to local thrift stores, and generally get some sort of normalcy back to life at home. I had wound my way back to my safe within my safe.

This is an old gray cash box with a little rinky-dink key lock on it that you could probably just stare at long enough and get it to unlock; thus why it's inside the 'real' safe. But this is where I keep the things that are truly most precious to me. Most of the contents are old birthday cards, letters, and pictures from my family -- the kind of things that no matter how old you get, still can bring a tear to your eye. There are a few other things, like extra copies of my final will, but for the most part, its cards and letters.

Then I picked up an envelope I hadn't remembered being in there. It was a three-page autobiography I had written my junior year in high school. It was dated December 13, 1996 -- almost 16 years ago to the day. I opened it and read it while sitting on my recliner, with my dog Tripper (aka Doodle) who was guarding my faux suede, faux sheepskin (and probably faux rubber) slippers. Kohl's clearance -- practically faux free.

It was a bit nostalgic to read a letter I had written and completely forgotten about, but in three pages, it was a fairly general autobiography.

I mean, how much detail can you really give on sixteen or seventeen years of life in three pages?

Then I got to the final paragraph, which reads as follows:

"What is to become of my life from this point on is yet to be determined by God and quite honestly, I do not wish to know what is going to happen with my life. This makes my decisions and responsibility that much more important. I cannot merely exist just to exist; I need to serve a purpose in life whether I become a role model to a nation or to a single person. Whatever I become, whatever my future may be, I hope I am able to use my talents to their fullest to benefit others."

My body began shaking and tears streamed down my face. I fell face down on the floor and spoke the only thing that I could think to say, "You knew God -- You knew. You really do know my end from its beginning don't You?"

18

MEXICAN FRIDAY

Friday, December 14, 2012

Trey's Dad, Loren, and I made plans to meet on Friday for lunch at La Parilla, a Mexican restaurant just south of Gainesville. When I made plans for lunch, I had completely forgotten that I'd already committed to dinner plans with some friends Friday night at El Jimador, a Mexican restaurant just north of Gainesville. So needless to say, somewhere in the following 24hrs, there was the reenactment of the Spanish-American War.

We sat down in a corner booth and over the course of the next half-hour, I gave him the short and skinny on the last four months of my life. As I wrapped up the part about Perry's book, Loren took a bathroom break. As he got up and walked off, I just sat there thinking about all that was happening. "You can't make this stuff up!" I thought to myself.

Then the guy in the booth in front of me, who was sitting on the opposite side of the booth (facing my direction) peers around his lunch companion and says, "You have some pretty dangerous company for lunch". I thought he was talking to someone else. Then he makes eye contact with me again and says the same thing again -- followed by "I thought I heard you talking about Uganda." I looked at him, never having laid eyes on this person before, and said "Uhh, yeah." He just looked at me with a pensive gaze and kind of lifted his head a little bit and said "Huh."

Solid interchange so far, right?!

Then Loren walks back, sees me with this puzzled look on my face, directing my gaze towards the next booth, and turns to look at the other half of my recent conversation, and says, "Hey David! What are you doing here?"

As it happened, the other guy, David, is on the Board of Directors for the mission's organization Loren is a part of: Helping Hands Foreign Missions. So Loren starts to introduce me to David, and after about fifteen seconds, David looks at me and says, "Do you have any construction experience?"

I sat there dumbfounded. "Uhh… yeah – wuhhh -- why?" He just looked at me the same way as before, lifting his head a little, and said "Huh".

So Loren continues the introduction, telling David and his lunch companion that I work up at The Simpson Company in Gainesville. The lunch companion looks up at Loren and says, "The Simpson Company? That's where my wife works."

I am not believing my ears.

"Wwwww… wait -- what?!" I exclaimed in disbelief. "Who's your wife?" I said in astonishment to the back of his head.

He turns halfway around so I just get a glimpse of his mustache (which was awesome by the way), and says "Kelly"

Kelly is our Office Manager.

I leaned my head against the side of the booth in disbelief and laughed. "God," I thought, "You really are making this idiot-proof aren't You?!"

19

"ALL THE KIDS LOVE MR. JAKE"

Sunday, December 16, 2012

It's a dreary Sunday and I begin walking down the church hallway leading to the Snail Room back in Kids Cove. The Kids Cove staff puts on a volunteer appreciation breakfast a couple times a year, just as a 'Thank You', which happens to be this morning. So I stop in, pick up an array of breakfast items and then head on back to my room.

The morning's pretty typical. Probably about fifteen kids or so back in our area; that's about the norm this time of year. We get everyone distracted from Mom & Dad departing and settled in to playing, then saddle up ten of them between two of our "Bye-Bye-Buggy's"; which are essentially giant plastic stroller-buses. Whenever we mention "Bye-Bye-Buggy" to the kids, they start flocking like lemmings to the area where they are stored. They may not be able to communicate that well verbally yet, but they understand the code name for 'souped-up-plastic-mobiles'.

Denny (one of the other volunteers back in our area) takes the six-seater and I take the four-seater and off we go to do a couple laps around the church hallways. I normally try to take some time on the journey around the church to stop and point out simple things, as a means of bringing some degree of education to the trip for the kids. For example, being a few weeks before Christmas, I'll stop in front of one of the Christmas trees, walk around from the back of the Bye-Bye-Buggy so the kids can see me, and ask the kids if anyone sees a Christmas Tree?

Normally I get 4-6 blank stares. Sometimes one of them will point, but normally I get the "Hey… how 'bout you get back in line and push this thing" stare. So I then do the cheesy Sesame Street, "This is a Chriiiiiisssttmmaass Trreeeee" point and slowly repeat deal.

Blank stares.

The stares are quickly followed by looks of inquiry; heads tilting slightly as to insinuate, "Aaaaand who told you to stop pushing this thing?"

So we wrap up our ride and get the kids in the table-highchair-insert-seats for snack time.

As I'm getting my kids in their seats, Denny comes over to my room and out of the blue says, "You know Jake, you should open up a day-care or something… make a living out of this. You've got a gift. All the kids love Mr. Jake."

Now, it's ok for kids to cry in Kids Cove. It's not ok for adults to. I tried to just pass off the compliment with an "oh, yeah, it's fun isn't it" or something like that -- trying to avoid eye contact so I wouldn't erupt into tears. I mean, how do you tell someone, out of the blue, "Yeah, you don't know it, but you are just one in a long line of people and things confirming what God is doing in my life. He's sending me to Uganda, a country I've never set foot in -- didn't even know where it was a couple months ago, and that's about all the details He's shared with me at this point. Now hold this kid while I go find a paci and have myself a good cry."

Denny and I have worked together back in Kids Cove for two years and not once has either of us said anything to each other like this. It's just not something guys normally do… it's like talking in the men's bathroom; you just don't do it. There was nothing different about this morning and I don't really know what possessed Denny to say that to me this particular morning other than God knows my faith has tested in the 'special-needs' category (no offense… I'm just the world's best second-guesser) on more than one occasion and He's taking extra measures to ensure I'm handled as such.

20

THE SEED SOWN

Friday, December 21, 2012

It's the last day, well… half-day, of work before going on a week and a half trip to see my family up in Pennsylvania. It's a relatively typical Friday morning aside from the gale force winds outside. I'd been to the gym before work and sat at my desk sipping my normal cup of coffee while scanning through my email Inbox and reviewing some paperwork that needed to be signed off on before I head out of town.

One of the things I left out earlier, when I started getting a strong sense and some initial confirmation in October and November that God was sending me to Uganda, I mention here only to show God's remarkable faithfulness to His Word; He means what He says, regardless of whether or not we choose to believe it enough to act on it.

I had felt this… I don't know, just this weird sense from God to test Him on all this stuff. I mean, this is all *still* so much to take in. Yet God gives us very clear direction in The Bible on testing Him. There's one, and only one, way that God tells us to test Him; giving.

This probably sounds a bit bizarre (what doesn't at this point?), but I felt like God was telling me to "sow a seed" if you will, into Katie's ministry. A specific dollar amount popped into mind when I initially prayed about it. Frankly, it was a bit large for my comfort and budget -- about three times the amount I tithe to my church in a given month. One of the largest single donations I'd ever made and during a time and season where I'm not exactly rolling in cash. I don't know how else to describe it other than I felt like God saying to me, "Hey, you want to test Me and see if this is Me? Put the seed in the field. Let it go into the ground in Uganda. And wait."

I bring this up only because of this:

On December 21st, my boss walks in to my office as I'm doing my normal Friday morning deal and has this strange facial expression I can't really read, puts his briefcase down next to my door, and then closes the door to my office behind him.

"Rut-row" I thought to myself.

He then proceeds to shower a few compliments on me about the job I've done over the last year or so and then pulls out from inside his blazer a yellow envelope and hands it to me. It was filled with large bills. I sat there totally overwhelmed. I thanked him, we chit-chatted a few minutes, and then he went on with getting his day started.

I didn't count the money in the office -- I just felt awkward doing that. The only people I can think of that count large bills in their office are bankers and the mob. Insert your own joke here. So I drove over to my bank about an hour later, parked, and fished out the envelope.

I counted it.

I couldn't believe it.

Almost one month to the day from when I 'sowed' the seed, I now held in my hands *exactly two-times* the amount I had sown into Katie's ministry. This is/was the first year-end bonus I've ever received in over ten years in the 'professional' world, working for a real estate company... in Georgia... which is either #1 or #2 in "hardest hit real estate markets in the United States" during the economic recession.

Stupid is the word you're probably looking for... stupid-awesome is this God.

That night, with a huge smile inside of me, I got to put another seed in the ground in Uganda.

21

THE TALK

Saturday, December 22, 2012

As I woke up for my drive home to Pennsylvania and see the family for Christmas, it dawned on me that I had just survived the Mayan Apocalypse. Talk about lucky!

Bags were packed so Tripper and I got on the road amidst thirty-to-forty mile per hour winds and snow through a good portion of the first few hours of darkness on our drive. There's no better way to wake up in the morning than running on low sleep and white-knuckling the steering wheel while it snows sideways. Starbuck's has a drink for that. It's called the "double-we're-closed-achino".

I figured either today or tomorrow (Sunday) I was going to have to break the news about all this to my immediate family. To this point, the only thing I had said to any of them was back in early November, when I remember talking on the phone with my mom.

I was in the parking lot of a local Goodwill Store when she called. I remember telling her that I was feeling like God might be leading me in a new direction in general and just wanted some specific prayer for discernment. That was literally all I had said to her. The last thing I wanted to do at this juncture in my life was be hasty or foolish. Then, earlier this week, I had sent her a short email and told her I wanted to have some time this weekend to talk with just her and Bob. I wanted to get them up to speed before breaking any news to my siblings.

As it happened, one of my sisters, Jamie, was heading out Saturday night for a Christmas party, and the other, Julie, was going to one on the following night (Sunday). So I figured I'd go ahead and get the cards on the table with Julie present and then talk with Jamie sometime Sunday.

After dinner, amidst a quivering chin and a few tears, I shared with my mom, Bob, and Julie what all God had been doing the last few months. I didn't share the level of detail that I've written about here, but covered the major stuff. When I was finishing up the story, I recounted to my mom this time in November when I had asked for prayer regarding discernment, stating that I'd got a little more than I was expecting.

She looks at Bob and said she remembered me asking for that specific prayer. Then, when they received my email earlier this week stating I wanted to have some individual time to talk, Bob apparently says to my mom, "I think he's either going to go into full-time ministry or going to become a missionary." Then Bob looks at my mom at the dinner table and says "And what did you say?"

"Missionary" she says

Understand this: I've *never* said anything to *anyone* -- EVER about being a missionary prior to this.

They share that with me at the end of our conversation -- which at this point I think is absolutely hilarious.

"Then what on earth are you so upset about?!" I said jovially. "Apparently you knew before I said anything".

Moms have a hard time letting go, even if their kids are grown-and-gone.

So... if someone told you they wanted prayer for discernment because they felt like God might be moving them in a different direction and then seven weeks later said they wanted to talk to you 'one-on-one' -- and that was literally all they'd said to you (beyond normal 'how was your week' conversation) -- would the first thought you had be "I'll bet they're going to tell me God's calling them to be some sort of missionary."

Is this not a little much?

22

THE NINE MONTH
OLD DEVOTION

Friday, December 28, 2012

Wednesday and Thursday, December 26th – 27th, were extremely difficult days. I won't go into all the details; we'll just call it dealing with some of the 'collateral damage' from a failed marriage.

Aside from August 4th, I don't know that there's a recent memory of when I was at a deeper low. I had literally cried for hours Wednesday and Thursday afternoon. All my siblings, their families and significant others, extended family -- everybody's home together and all I wanted was to be alone and try to sort out the emotional turmoil inside. Talk about feeling like a party-pooper.

I don't remember when during the day, but I had pulled up my email on my iPhone and saw that one of the men in my small group, Bob, had sent me an email with "Uganda" in the subject line.

I'd left he and his wife, Sue, a copy of this story (up to December 16th) before I left town, so I wasn't overly surprised at the subject line. Then I read the content of his email -- and laughed yet again. Below is the part of his email that caused my head to shake itself one more time and laugh to myself.

"Looked up Uganda on my atlas in fear that it might be on the coast of Africa and you might get taken there in the belly of a giant fish! Just another Kingdom Connection to add to your list - about a week ago Sue had an April

2012 edition of In-Touch Magazine *[note... this edition is 9 months old at this point]* lying around all by itself and, in my morning quiet time, I picked it up and read the article about Katie Davis. When I got home I told Sue and Lisa (daughter) to read it because it meant so much to me and Katie looked almost identical to Lisa in some of the photos. Then a couple of days later I read your booklet and was surprised to read of your spiritual connection with Katie's work in Uganda. Happy to see my God answers prayers for clarification - especially for something as drastic but exciting as you are going to be doing. Look forward to giving you a proper send-off. God Bless You Brother!"

23

THE SOFA TABLE
CONUNDRUM

Thursday, January 3, 2013

When I had lunch with Loren the other week at La Parilla, he had shared with me a little booklet entitled "Village of Eden: The Unfolding Miracle Continues". Helping Hands Foreign Missions had put together this booklet to explain and visually depict the different avenues and arenas this project in Uganda is covering. The project, as you might guess, is called the Village of Eden. It is effectively a village they have plans to construct across 130 acres, complete with a church, orphanages, a school, cultivated farm land, fish ponds, and a market (among other things). The Village of Eden is one of those things you look at and think, "If God's not behind this and in this, it ain't happening." It's a HUGE endeavor.

Village of Eden – January 2013

So today I'm taking the owners of a new vendor, a cleaning/janitorial company, through one of the larger bank buildings our company manages; meeting all the office managers and key people to answer questions and get the new guys off on the right foot. There's a wide range of commercial tenants in the building; everything from non-profits, to various professional services, to doctor's offices.

As we wrap up, I'm walking our new vendor through the last office; an attorney's office on the third floor. As I'm going through the lobby to show them into the spacious conference room behind the half-inch thick glass doors that greet the entrance, I notice a cherry-finished sofa table to the left of the door with a fake plant on it. I've been in this office probably twenty or thirty times over the last year and a half -- never noticed the table before. Honestly, how often do you actually look at stuff like this in other people's offices? Most of us can't recall what color the walls are in our *own* office.

Next to the fake plant are a stack of little booklets, which read "Village of Eden: The Unfolding Miracle Continues". I can't write what the first thought I had in my head. Let's just say I think God laughed out loud.

At this point, you're probably thinking, "Wow Jake, God must think you're really blind, really deaf, and mentally-challenged if He's dropping all this on you like this?" For the first few months, that's exactly what I thought. But as I have kept asking for more, each step of confirmation drawing me closer to Him and further into this journey, I had another thought enter my mind, which frankly, brings tears to my eyes every time I think of it.

I believe God is providing all this confirmation because He is preparing, or has prepared, something much bigger than I can imagine or handle. I fully acknowledge that all this is not normal -- as I am becoming increasingly aware that what God is calling me into is equally abnormal. I believe He is, in a sense, giving me the foundation of confirmation (that I'll admit, is a bit over-the-top), because the road ahead is going to be more challenging -- the calling, work, and vision far bigger -- and the faith requirements far greater, than probably anything I've ever known.

That both thrills the heck out of me and scares me to death.

24

THE INVITATION

Sunday, January 6, 2013

Yesterday (Saturday) was paint & mulch day.

In getting the house ready to put on the market, two of my more significant projects were painting over a big red wall inside the house and putting a fresh layer of mulch down outside. The brown mulch was delivered in the morning, complete with a fresh dose of steam from the cold temperatures outside. I got the red wall taped off, painted, and touched up by mid-afternoon, so I decided even though I wouldn't be able to get even half the mulching done, I'd go ahead and start.

In the process of putting the mulch down, I had dug up a few things that I threw in my wheelbarrow to go dump over in the woods at the side of the yard, where dead plants go to die their second death. I have a fifty-five gallon metal barrel on the side of the yard that I burn things in from time to time. I had burned a bunch of boxes and a few rotten logs from the firewood stack this past Monday (six days prior) after returning home from Christmas break. Tuesday, New Year's Day, it was a banner "tomato soup and grilled cheese" day -- chilly and rainy all day long.

As I passed by the burn barrel, I thought while I was in my 'yard clothes', I'd go ahead and empty the barrel out and put it on its side so it didn't gather any more water. Several times before I'd forgotten to turn it over and, let's just say, in its current location and being partially full of water, it becomes quite weighty and cumbersome to maneuver. As I turned the barrel over and then upside down, a big dust and ash cloud arose, so I quickly pulled the barrel away and stowed it away behind a big oak tree nearby. I opted to go on inside for a quick snack, thinking as I walked in, how much I loved the smell of wood ash and fires in the winter.

Someone should invent a "Campfire Musk" cologne.

I'd buy it just to smell myself.

A few minutes later, I grabbed my gloves and pitchfork and began loading up another wheelbarrow full of mulch. As I turned down the driveway to deliver the mulch to the landscape bed by the mailbox, I took a whiff of the glorious campfire smell again. Then something caught the corner of my eye. I turned my gaze over to the side yard and stared in disbelief. A small, but noticeable plume of white smoke was trailing up into the wind. I said out loud, but to no audience, "There's no way! There's no freaking way anything's still smoldering." I dropped off the loaded wheelbarrow at the end of the driveway and then went to have a closer look. I couldn't believe it. There were still a few small pieces of cardboard – *cardboar* -- that glowed red and pink as a light breeze hit the ash pile.

I stared in absolute disbelief for about thirty seconds, scratched the noggin', and went back to spread the mulch that I'd left in the wheelbarrow. Every other time we have received a day of rain, there's generally at least a few inches of water in the barrel. Yet this not only appeared to be not wet, but was *still smoldering*! As I started unloading the wheelbarrow, I shook my head and said a very unassuming, but direct prayer. "God, there is no way there should be anything warm, not to mention actually still smoldering in that pile… and certainly not *cardboard*! It rained for practically twenty-four hours straight five or six days ago. There's always standing water in that barrel after a rain like that. So what's the deal? I mean seriously -- is there something You want to show me in this, as dumb as that may sound? So what is it?"

This is honestly how I pray sometimes.

Then, out of left field, like someone smacking me in the back of the head, my 'life verse' popped right in front of my eyes. This was a verse that I stumbled upon around the time I felt God put a calling to full-time ministry on my life back in the summer of 2003. The verse is Romans 11:29, which says very simply, "For God's gifts and His calling are irrevocable." Simple translation: once God assigns us gifts to be used for His work, He assigns a place, or avenue, for those gifts to be used for His Kingdom -- neither of which He will ever take back. It is, in modern economic terms, sort of like a trust; assets for a designated purpose.

As I emptied the wheelbarrow, I felt like the message was loud and clear: "Son, all the gifts and abilities I've bestowed on you and equipped you with have been to prepare you for this, but it's your choice to go and use them. If you choose not to, I'll send someone else, but I'm not removing the calling you're seeing laid out before you. It will be there the rest of your life -- smoldering. Your choice."

That was yesterday.

This morning, I'm having my quite time before church in my brown recliner; coffee in my left hand, Tripper lying by my right side. The recliner is the only piece of furniture she's allowed up on, in case you're wondering if I'm one of those people who drive around with three dogs sticking their heads out of the front driver's side window while barreling down the highway, endangering all of humanity in the process. I'm not that guy (and you shouldn't be either).

This particular morning though, Tripper keeps giving me "the butt-jab", trying to push me over and jockey for more real estate on the chair. Perhaps she thinks it's her chair that she's letting me sit on it?

What a typical morning 'quiet time' looks like

Anyway, as part of what I'm currently reading in the Old Testament, I'm going through the book of Esther. This morning I'm reading chapter four. To summarize where we're at here, Haman (bad guy in the story) has convinced King Xerxes to issue an edict that in effect will result in the extermination of the Jews. Esther (who is Jewish) is in the palace of the king at this point as one of his harem and her uncle, Mordecai, is back at his home in the city. That's the scene we enter in chapter four.

Esther sends a messenger to Mordecai to see what can be done about this terrible situation all her family, friends, and community are now in. Honestly, just think of this: a law has been passed that gives the local police the legal right to kill basically everyone you know and love. A jacked up, gut-wrenching circumstance if there ever was one. But Mordecai dispatches the messenger back to Esther with this basic message, "Look, God has placed you inside the palace, at this point in Jewish history, with direct access to the king, for such a time as this; to speak up and act on behalf of your people. Yes, you entering the king's presence, without being summoned by him, may result in your death (as was often the case). *But if you don't do this*, if you choose to remain silent and not act, God will send someone else who is willing to lay it all on the table for His people. Your choice."

And like the snap of the fingers, God brought my mind back to yesterday, in effect saying, "If you don't go, if you choose to remain where you're at and not to step out, I'll send someone else. My plans cannot and will not be thwarted by the disobedience of one person. My invitation is to you, but the choice is yours to accept it."

25

OF COURSE IT DID

Saturday, January 26, 2013

On Monday, January 14th, I put my house on the market. As I had been praying and journaling, this was one of the main challenges I set before God. Note -- not prayer requests. I wrote out His challenges if He really wanted to send me to Uganda. Why? Because He is able. God says He is able to meet all my challenges and needs according to His riches which are in and through Christ.

I literally remember shrugging my shoulders and praying as I went into this decision, "Look God, this is Your house to begin with. You want to sell it and get this ball rolling, then You'll have to do it. January is probably the second worst month to list a house (behind December), but I'm guessing You know that. The only homes to sell in my neighborhood in the last three years, with the exception of one that didn't go on the market, have been foreclosures... and I'm guessing You know that as well. But *none of this*, thus far, has been anything I've had much of a hand in orchestrating or initiating, so if this is something You want to do, here's the challenge God -- sell Your house."

Four days later, the buyers walked through my front door. His house went under contract today. The closing is set almost exactly one month before I land in Uganda for the very first time.

In-sane.

26

ONE PHONE CALL

Monday, January 28, 2013

So when my agent sent me a text message to tell me the house was officially under contract, she asked, "So where are you moving to in February?"

Ha...

Huh...

Hmm...

Uhh.

That is a great question.

My human-nature was tempted to go into mild-freak-out mode; sort stuff to yard sale, have said yard sale, pack everything else, maintain my job, find place to live, wear clean clothes -- you have 30days -- aaaand GO! But I honestly had to laugh at myself as my logistics/planning pyramid started to topple over. "God just put your house from 'on the market' to 'under contract' in less than two weeks. You think he's going to put you out on the street?"

When we started the offer-counteroffer game last week, I thought to myself, "Ok, what would be ideal for me, if in fact God is sending me to Uganda in the near future?"

Somewhere inexpensive, quiet, and close to work. That would be ideal.

On the route I drive to and from the office every day, I pass about four or five blocks of 1970-1980's era four-plexes and small single-family homes before you get to the commercial buildings. This area, I thought, would be perfect. There were two or three "For Rent" signs out along the street, so I called the first and left a message for a "Scotty". As I began calling the number for the second place, I realized it was the same number as the first, so I figured I'd just wait for Scotty to call me back.

Around 5:00pm that afternoon I have an incoming call from a law firm our company just engaged to help with a couple things at one of our properties. I answered, expecting to hear my new contact at the firm, only to hear, "Jake? Hey this is Scotty. You left a message about some rental property I have here in Gainesville earlier."

"Yeah," I said kind of startled, "Sorry, I saw the caller ID and thought this was Rustin." I went on to tell Scotty about our work with their firm, at which point he says something about how he knows my boss from church.

"Your church?" I said "I go to the same church as my boss -- you go to Lakewood?"

"Yeah, you do too?" he said.

"Yeah, I volunteer back in Kids Cove for the first service and then go to the second service" I responded.

"You do?" he said laughingly, "My wife and I volunteer back in Kids Cove for the first service and we go to the second service too. My wife works back with the infants -- and I help teach a 10th grade guys Sunday school class -- with your boss Frank".

Of course he does, right?!

The one phone number I saw and called on a street corner in Gainesville ends up being someone whose wife I've known for two years and 'happens' to not only go to my church, but teach Sunday School class with my boss. I felt like breaking into the 1984 one-hit-wonder by Rockwell, "I always feel like, somebody's watching me". Oh -- by the way -- guess which closing attorney in town the *buyers* chose to handle our closing? Yup. Scotty's firm.

Is this not certifiably ridiculous at this point?

27

THE 'IT'

Wednesday, February 6, 2013

Loren had been in back in the states for about a week or so from his latest trip to Uganda when I sent him a text message about trying to get together for lunch and talk things over. We met at a tiny little Chinese restaurant in Oakwood. Note to self -- never, never, never order "sweet tea" in a Chinese restaurant. Never. I'll leave it at that.

So Loren and I sit down in a booth. We comprised about fifty percent of the restaurants clientele at that point for the lunch hour, so it was an ideal environment for conversation.

We opened the conversation talking about the mission trip to Uganda I'd committed to go on with Helping Hands. I told him in conjunction with that, I'd felt distinctly impressed to build a portable 'puppet stage' out of PVC that could collapse down and fit into a duffel bag. I know this is kind of a weird thing to bring up in conversation, but I felt like I was supposed to share that with him -- hoping he wouldn't think I was a complete fruitcake after hearing this. I'd ordered five hand puppets from Amazon.com and was working with a friend to design the 'scene/stage'. Please understand, I know this sounds *WEIRD*. But I'm telling you -- before I built the thing, I saw it in my mind clear as day. I'd never seen one like this before, but I knew the approximate dimensions -- somehow.

The frame (about half way through the process)

One of my talents, as I've been told by a couple friends that know me very well, is that I can do "voices" really well. Not a ton in my repertoire, but five or so which are really solid and comical. My buddy Lucas and I used to make 'pride-bets' when we were roommates and were broke. We didn't have money to bet, so we'd wager our pride. A common wager was that the next time we were at a restaurant, the loser had to order and converse with the waiter/waitress in an accent/voice of the winners choosing. The catch was that the loser was never allowed to explain to the poor waiter/waitress what was going on. And it seemed like I lost a lot. And as my pride diminished with each bet, I developed better voices.

Some people are talented in mathematics and go to places like Princeton University. They do so well and are so talented at what they do, they then go to work for NASA as a Flight Controller for the International Space Station. That would be my friend and classmate from high school, Ken. Others have a really savvy business mind and a personality that screams 'success'. Upon completing their undergrad at Georgia Tech, they attend the University of Florida to get their prestigious MBA. But they are so talented, they then get their PhD from the University of Central Florida while they are working as young executive for Disney -- at Disney. That would be another classmate and friend of mine from high school, Bo. Me? God gave me the knack for puppet voices. Yay... for... me.

Back to lunch at the Chinese restaurant. Loren responds to this seemingly random/weird comment from me about the puppet stage, not by saying, "Are you on crack?" or "So I've been meaning to talk to you about how we process our background checks" like you might expect, but "one of the pastors I spoke with in Uganda said to me that he would really like to figure out some way to integrate puppets into reaching out to the community's children, but hasn't had the time, staff, or resources yet".

I looked Loren straight in the eyes and said, "Shut... up. You have got to be freaking kidding me?!" Understand: this thing was not somewhere in my brain -- it was in my garage, already built. The puppets? Not in my 'wish list' cart on Amazon.com. They were in my pantry. I felt like my soul had just licked a car battery. I can truly identify with Steve Carell's character in the movie *Evan Almighty* -- you just feel like an absolute idiot until the "ohhhhhh, thank God I'm not nuts" moment comes. Honestly, sometimes I feel like Jesus is just straight up messing with me, but then I remember that He does everything on purpose, for a purpose.

While I was doing all this, I literally felt like it was a miniature version of Noah's Ark. I mean, I don't -- didn't -- understand it *at all* while I was doing it. I can't tell you how many times I almost stopped and just said to myself, "Jake, seriously dude -- this may be *the dumbest thing you have EVER done*! Not only that, but this kind of 'weirdo-esk'. What in the heck are you doing?" Not while I was at Home Depot buying the PVC, not while I was shopping for puppets and mentally matching the voice with the right animal/character, not while I was piecing together the elbows, T's, and couplings to make sure the thing was sturdy and collapsible… nowhere in the process did I really know why or for what purpose I was doing this. But I could see the thing before I built it. I don't know how to describe it other than the analogy of Noah -- I simply felt like I had very specific instructions from God -- to build a stinkin' puppet stage and order some puppets. Yeah, you figure that one out.

And then it happened. Loren immediately launched into the question at hand.

"So since the last time we talked, have you heard back from Katie's ministry?" he asked. When we had parted after lunch at La Parilla the other month, his last comment to me was that he was praying God would make my way clear to me and then as a semi-joking aside, "But selfishly I hope it's not with Katie's ministry".

"No," I replied, "I've contacted them twice and haven't heard a word back. I don't know -- part of my prayer through this whole process has been that God would make whatever direction He's sending me obvious. I have no idea what He's doing -- what He's preparing. I just regularly tell Him 'Hey, I'll do whatever You want, but You better make it clear because I have no idea what I'm doing'. You know -- just praying for His opening and closing of doors. There's still time between now and when I get to Uganda in April, but I'm beginning to believe God may have closed that door."

Loren tried to not look a little excited about that, but I could tell something was up.

"So Trey (his son) and I talked and he said you were planning on going out with him on the mission trip and then staying an extra week." he said with a degree of eagerness. "Could you come earlier?"

"What do you mean 'earlier'?" I asked.

"Well," he replied, "I'm going out on March 19th before the group gets there. That's about ten days before Trey's group arrives. If it's at all possible, I'd like you to come out with me and meet the team out there and give them some time to meet you before everyone else arrives."

Then he said "it".

The "it" that I believe has been in the works through the ways and means only God could have orchestrated these last six months or so.

"We've been praying for an American man with building or construction experience to oversee the building of the Village of Eden."

He paused.

"I think you might be that person and I'd like to give both you and the team in Uganda some time to see if this is in fact the right fit."

Honestly, I just about threw my hands up and said, "of course that's what you've been praying for?! I bet the Lord told you your guy was going to be about 5'9" tall, brown hair, and currently works in real estate, right!"

I recalled what I'd written earlier -- that all of this stuff God was doing was not normal -- thus my conclusion: the task/calling/mission must be equally abnormal.

Help build a literal village in east Africa. LOL... ok... if You say so.

With all the stuff that had happened at this point in the story, I had journeyed (or trudged) through the fact that even in my darkest times, God is faithful to walk beside me and sustain me. Not that He was 'worried' about it, but He had earned a new, more tangible, level of trust in my life -- simply by being who He is -- the same as He was yesterday and will be forever.

The second song that intersected my life, somewhere around January, is David Crowder's "Sometimes". If you look up the lyrics, it's almost laughable:

> "Sometimes. every one of us feels, like we'll never be healed" (like surviving a divorce)
>
> "Risk the ocean" (like the Atlantic perhaps?)
>
> "Where you go we will follow" (like to Uganda perhaps?
>
> "Oh God send me" (like… uhh… me?).

I mean, imagine living this story out and then one day you download this song on iTunes solely because you love the artist, and kah-blam -- grab a napkin -- you've been served.

So since I issued God His three challenges back in December, within the first sixty days, He has seemingly answered two of the three in a fashion that I think I'll dub "divine pizazz".

God is zazzy.

28

SELLING MISSIONARY
HOUSES = EASY MONEY

Monday, February 25, 2013

Over the course of the last month or so, I found out that my real estate agent was also a Believer. She kept asking me what my plans were for the future, "Where are you moving to?" I kept 'hemmin-and-hawin' around the subject because I didn't want to say something out of tune with what God was doing or get out of line with His timing.

So I told her last week that I would leave her the story of what God had been working out over the last few months, expressed my appreciation, and said that I was glad she was able to be a part of the story.

Today she picked up the story and read it while she was at the gym. This is the content of her text message that was sent after she read it:

> "Read the whole thing… He is worthy of all honor and praise! I know He is faithful. Of all the houses our company has listed in the last year, only three have sold within the first week [mine being the 3rd]. All three owners were selling their homes to get involved in missionary work."

At this point, I am honestly more fearful of staying in the US than I am of facing Yellow Fever, Typhoid, Malaria, Polio, HIV/AIDS, and ill-tempered baboons. The God who created life simply by saying, "Let there be" appears to have a target on me and as incredible as this has all been, it's a tidbit scary too. I don't know what else to make of this. I know some might say, "Well, you can serve God in all sorts of ways. You don't necessarily have to go all the way to Uganda." That philosophy didn't work out too well for Jonah.

I am in the process of understanding, in a whole new way, what David meant when he said, "The fear of the Lord is the beginning of wisdom" in Psalm 111:10. No I'm not claiming galactic wisdom resides in me, but generally speaking, it's going to be a bad day if I know I'm not obeying specific direction from the One who made the first quasar and set the first supernova in motion.

29

.13 PERCENTILE

Friday, March 8, 2013

I had made plans to meet up with my buddy, Justin, for breakfast at Chick-Fil-A in town. Justin is one of those guys who my spirit and his just connect. We may not see each other for a long time, but when we get together, it's like no time has passed -- we just pick up like we saw each other last week. He's an associate pastor now and serves as a chaplain in the US Army reserves. He is unconventional, has no boxes he really fits into, loves his family, loves Jesus, has access to automatic weapons, and gave me his receipt with the "Fill this survey out and get a free Chick-Fil-A Sandwich" coupon on it.

We need more Justin's in this world.

I had brought him a couple copies of this book at that point in the story and we spent the hour catching up on life. I like to sit in what I call the "covert booth" at this Chick-Fil-A because the booth is hidden from view from the majority of the restaurant. It is next to the kids play area, which I would go into except for the fact that I think I'd get stuck inside the plastic gerbil tubes -- my "turning radius" isn't what it used to be.

As we were talking and catching up, two moms came and sat down in the booth right behind Justin's side of our booth. During our conversation, the mom facing my direction did this little side-look-around thing in my direction. I figured she was probably looking out in the parking lot for a third mom or something; thought nothing of it.

So we get up to leave. Justin, having been caught up on the contents of this book, is reeling at the ridiculousness of the confirmation and presence of God in all that has transpired. We turn to walk past the mom-booth, when the 'look-around' mom motions to me and says, "Hey... did you write a book?"

Justin looks at me with the same look I've been wearing for the last few months. I grab one of the books I'd given him and say, "You mean this?"

"Yeah, that's it! Do you know CJ?" she asks.

CJ is/was my realtor.

This woman is the wife of CJ's pastor, who she'd given a copy of this to.

Understand... there are about 183,000 people in my county -- Hall County, GA -- which is roughly a fifteen mile radius around this Chick-Fil-A. I had given out somewhere maybe 250 of these at this point. This woman is in 0.13 percentile of the geographic population that has knowledge of this story.

So in case you have been calculating the odds of all this stuff happening to me, start at 0.13% and work your way down.

30

TIME-CHALLENGED

Saturday, March 9, 2013

So, in case you're wondering, what's the 3ʳᵈ challenge you gave God back in December? Here it is. I am part owner of a timeshare at a Marriott in Aruba. Without going into the details, my prayer challenge was very simply that God would provide a 'renter' for this year and hopefully sell it, as it is currently up for sale. I intentionally have not mentioned this because "timeshare" has such an unsavory ring to it for most people. I won't go into too many details, but will share a couple things that are pertinent, which all timeshare folks know to be true:

1. Almost without exception, you have to book your vacation a minimum of 6mo's in advance -- usually more like a year in advance. Inside of 90 days? You can forget about it.
2. If you rent it out, 95% of renters are looking with the 30-120day window, which makes renting your week out rather challenging based on Rule #1.
3. Everyone wanting to rent your week wants a Saturday-to-Saturday check-in.
4. The timeshare booking people almost never have the Saturday-to-Saturday check-in dates you want.

I have the timeshare listed on a website I used last year to rent the week [redweek.com... well worth checking out if you're looking for a great deal on prime vacation spots]. It seemed to work pretty well and was relatively easy, so I figured I'd give it another go. Late last night (Friday 3/8), I get an email from someone looking to potentially rent the week. They're requesting *Thursday*, May 16th for check-in -- just over sixty days. Ugh. I figured I'd at least give the folks at Marriott a call and see, rolling my eyes as the thought went through my head.

Tripper (I call her Doodle most of the time) and I were going out for another hike after her annual check-up at the vet. My vet and I ended up discussing what all God's been doing with me in regards to Uganda, at which point, she informs me her son wants to be a missionary also as a bush pilot, flying missionaries into remote areas. We chit-chat a little, Doodle gets her shots and the usual "Hey! Whoa! What are you doing back there?" deal, I drop $100, and we're off to our hike.

Doodle at the vet… pre-shots & 'Whoa!'

So I called Marriott. Actually, I'd called them a couple weeks ago for someone else that was looking for a check-in date in June. No dice... not surprising. But I called anyway. The customer service person I spoke with was very nice, as they always are. I explained that I was looking to see if they had a specific date for a check-in. I winced, "in May" I said squeamishly.

"This May?" she said, with a raised eye brow I could see over the phone. "I doubt we'll have anything, but I'll look" she said.

"Yeah, I know there aren't really any odds I'm working with here," I said, thinking this is a thorough waste of time for both of us. "I figured I'd just call and verify anyway though."

"Oh," she said, "I do remember there being one cancellation made yesterday for May I think. Let me see -- where was it -- yes, looks like we have one check-in available in May... [drum roll]... Thursday, May 16th is our only availability in May. Do you want to book it?"

"No I'll just call back later"

No I didn't really say that.

I reserved the week for the renter, had the cash in my PayPal account within an hour, and sent him an email with the confirmation information for the reservation. I figured I'd tell the renter the property was up for sale if they were interested, I'd make a good deal with them. I got a call back from the guy about thirty minutes later, thanking me for the smooth transaction and letting me know that he goes down to Aruba almost every year and would definitely be interested in discussing the purchase when he got back in May.

Doodle and I on our hike that day.

31

THE HILARITY

There is really only one reason I'm including this 'chapter' in the book; because I think it's hilarious and I love to share laughter.

I arrived home tonight after one of the final sessions of my *Perspectives In Foreign Missions* classes. A church down the street was hosting it. There were people from all ages and church affiliations in the class. It's effectively a seminary level 'missions' class for those either going into missionary service in some capacity or are interested in learning more about it.

Doodle was cat-napping when I got home.

Shocker!

There were a couple things I had to take care of before bed, but ended up turning the sheets down around 10:45pm or so. I read a short chapter in a book I am slowly working my way through on my nightstand and then rolled over to call it a night. The dull orange glow provided by the outside street lights lit up just enough of the room for me to stare aimlessly at the faded plaster ceiling. I started thinking of all the things that are contained in this book -- and even a few more I haven't written about.

By 11:10pm, I was laughing hysterically.

I was actually in tears I was laughing so hard.

Doodle was probably thinking, "Oh boy... here goes the farm!" I have my hands over my face and I'm in absolute stitches. And I just asked God, "Do You really know what You are doing?" I wasn't asking in an accusatory or doubting sort of way; it was the sentiment of "God, really -- You want to use me over there? You realize it wouldn't be out of the question for me to cause some sort of international incident simply by -- being me, right?"

I literally felt like I was in a remake of the scene in Lethal Weapon 4 where Riggs & Murtaugh go in to question Uncle Benny, the Chinese mobster, in the dentist office. Uncle Benny is getting laughing gas for his procedure. The laughing gas mask gets removed from his face, the gas gets turned waaaaay up, and pretty soon both the questioner (me, in this instance) and the questioned (God) are both laughing hysterically. I know a lot of people don't think God finds anything funny or worth laughing about, but if He made us in His image and likeness, why wouldn't He laugh? This scene in Lethal Weapon 4 is one of the funniest scenes in an action movie that I've ever seen. I felt like God was laughing too; bent over, clutching His sides.

"I... I'm using the foo... foolish things of this world -- that's you Jake -- to confound the wwww... wise." Loud and clear; that's what I felt Him saying to me -- which made me convulse with laughter even more. I was shaking the bed I was laughing so hard. "Wwww... whelp" I said between breaths "Yyyy... You... hit the jackpot!" It still makes me laugh.

I grabbed my phone and pulled up one of the Bible apps on it. I looked up this passage in the New Testament, where it says that God uses the foolish things of this world to confound the wise, found in 1 Corinthians 1:27 and following. The Apostle Paul goes on to say that God also chooses the weak things of the world to shame the wise -- the things that are lowly of the world to nullify the things that are not -- *so that* no one, especially not me, may boast before God.

Paul says it is because of Christ that these things happen; so if we are to boast -- if I am to boast -- it is in Christ using someone as weak, lowly, and foolish as me to bring others the knowledge of the Gospel and the tangible love and power of Jesus -- alive and well in 2013.

32

A BRIEF PAUSE...
BRINGING IT HOME

Sunday, March 17, 2013

During one of the most painful seasons in my life, I have felt more joy, encouragement, and true communion with God than possibly any other time I can remember. Through the disillusionment of the first several months, and the various conversations I had with people 'checking in on me', there was one distinct emotion that I never felt.

Discouragement.

I had every reason to feel it, but I can recall numerous cups of coffee where I would literally sit there scratching my forehead and making a face like I was trying to solve an algorithm in my head, saying "I don't get it, but the one emotion I have not felt the slightest bit of is discouragement". It is *so* very odd to say that, but it is the absolute truth. I truly do not understand His ways or His plans -- heck, half the time, I think they flat out suck and could not be more backwards -- but I know these two things are certain:

1.   That God works *all things*, even death, divorce, abandonment, heartache, loss, abuse, and pain, for the good of those who love Him and are called according to His purpose.
2.   That He who began a good work in me nearly ten years ago, *can and will* carry it on to completion until the day I meet Jesus or He returns.

What God says, He does.

As much as I struggle with these over time, I cannot deny the calling God has laid within my heart. It's all I think about driving to and from work. It's what I have day-dreamed about for over nine years. It's what creates instant joy in my life. And I cannot deny His voice and presence these last few months. And therefore, I cannot not trust Him. Therefore I must go.

I full well realize to some degree this is completely nuts. I have read and re-read this story over countless times already. It… is… nuts. But I also realize that almost everything we see and read about in the Bible was, to some degree or another, completely nuts. I think that's God's point. We have a 3½lb brain to try and comprehend the thoughts and ways of a God who spoke and light somehow happened; if He always makes sense, He's too small to be a God I want any part of.

For the first few months, I tried to tell God how this was not the time nor was it a season in life to be making major changes -- how the wise thing to do is to regroup, stabilize, and rebalance things in life. Establish the 'new normal', get plenty of counseling, yadda yadda yadda.

As I perceive it, His response has been "The wise thing is to be obedient and do what I tell you and let me worry about the rest". Ever tried to refute that one?

I was driving home from church one night after having talked with one of the pastors at my church about all this. He said that his only concern was basically the timing of this in relation to the divorce. I essentially responded, "that makes two of us, but God doesn't appear to care or be listening to that argument."

I left church and drove home. As I was driving past one of the local red-brick elementary schools, I was re-hashing this conversation with God. "God… I agree with him on a certain level, but at the same time, what else can I make of all this?" And like the proverbial fly ball to deep centerfield to end the game, I felt one simple message from my Heavenly Father, "I Am the Lord. I… Am… The… Lord… that heals you. Not your church, not someone with a PhD, not Gainesville, and not proper timing. I am the One who heals you -- and I'm in Uganda no more or less than I am in Gainesville."

As best I can understand, it seems His two criteria are and have always been 'willing' and 'obedient'; it's the sentiment of "You provide the fire, I'll provide the sacrifice." I think that's what we see so clearly in the 'pillars' of faith as we know them -- Moses, Joseph, David, Samson, Elijah, Jonah, Peter and on and on -- laughingly, most of the main characters in the Bible. I read and consider what some of them did, said, and didn't do, and I think to myself, "Were you on crack?" By that same sentiment, I qualify to be used by God.

These people were really not your ideal candidates by any stretch of the imagination for writing a grand story about, but they had these two character traits in common. Seriously, if the Bible's made up of fictional stories, even half-truths, why on earth would you choose these people?! Moses couldn't run for an elected office in almost any country in the world because he was a *murderer*! These 'pillars' are like the *other* team the Harlem Globe Trotters play against -- the no-names. They were gravely imperfect, experienced colossal failures and errors in judgment, but they all returned to God as willing and obedient servants. God has all the resources in the world at His disposal; the *only* thing He does not have is our will to obey. When He is offered that, things start to happen. As Phil Robertson would say, "Now we're cooking with peanut oil!"

I see the inverse of this in Jesus' conversation with the "rich young ruler" in Mark 10. This guy seemingly 'did' everything the right way, but at his true core, he was neither obedient nor willing to follow the call of Jesus, and Jesus could do nothing with him or the resources he had been entrusted with. He exits the Gospel narrative, and world history for that matter, in sadness. The challenge I've had to wrestle with in all this is, "what differentiates my life from this guy's life?" I am both willing and obedient or I'm not. The Matrix had the blue pill or the red pill -- no purple pills. Two and only two options.

My one request of God, through this whole process, when I first sensed this was what God was doing, was that He would provide *abundant* confirmation, so that I would have no question whether or not this was Him. I can't just go 'just *to go*', there is too must risk and faith-challenges involved in that -- it is the breeding ground for doubt, discouragement, and epic failure. But if, God, I know that I am being *sent* -- I can have rest and peace that my feet are firmly fixed on the path laid out for me by my life's Grand Weaver. That was my request (actually, if I'm being honest, I kind of put it to Him as a demand more than a request), "God, I need to know I'm being sent. I can't just pick up and go, especially not no. I love Gainesville. I have a good, secure job. I am involved in a great church. I live in a beautiful house in an awesome part of the country. But if this is what You want, I am willing to be obedient -- but I need You to provide abundant confirmation so that there is no question in anyone's mind -- *especially mine*, that You are behind this." See what I'm talking about when I say 'special-needs' faith? But He is a loving Father, who knows how to give good gifts to His children that love Him and are actively seeking Him out.

Here's the comical thing to me; I've never thought about or really wanted to visit Africa, nor had I ever really desired to be any sort of missionary beyond going on a short-term mission trip. That just always seemed a little too Amish for me.

I lived in South Carolina for six years and Georgia for seven. I can't tell you how many times during those summers I've literally said these words to people: "I don't know how people live without air conditioning".

I love air conditioning.

I mean, I have actually hugged air conditioners before. You think I'm exaggerating? I have witnesses.

I love sweet tea. And I love Chick-Fil-A, which has both and air conditioning -- and brownies... oh man -- I really love brownies.

I recently visited a Chick-Fil-A and was told by the high school girl working the cash register that they no longer serve brownies. I literally collapsed on the counter next to the cash register. The poor girl didn't know what to do with that except to say, "But have you tried our cookies?"

Yes... I have. They're amazing. They'd be even more amazing if they were brownies.

Understand… I'm not fulfilling a life ambition of mine in any of this. Of my vacation destination spots/activities, the stereotypical 'African Safari' would rank somewhere between eight or nine on the list. And I'm not running from my life as I've known it. Aside from the heartache and loss that comes with a divorce, I love my life as-is. I'm just doing what I'm being told and trying to enjoy the ride and not fah-reak out.

For every question you would have for me, I have three.

Nervous? Uh der.

Fears? Just one (kinda huge one though). But so much excitement and anticipation.

I think this is probably one of the greatest tests of my resolve to not try and resolve the mind of God. David wrote in Psalm 37:4, saying, "Delight yourself in the Lord, and He will give you the desires of your heart." In many ways (which I won't go into here), having any involvement, whether it be 'moving-moving' to Uganda or some other sort of mission/ministry work in Uganda, it's the exact opposite direction of the desires of my heart. But if I know nothing else, I know that God is trustworthy and He always honors His Word.

I have no grand words of my own, but I think the words of the well-known missionary, David Livingstone, seem like a fitting entry into this chapter of my life…

> "Lord, send me anywhere, only go with me. Lay any
> burden on me, only sustain me. Sever any ties, but the
> ties that bind me to Your heart and Your service."

So I took the next step of what I believed to be obedience; I found Uganda on the map and sent the original copy of this to Katie Davis back in late November 2012. While I still don't have all the details, I'm confident of this:

God is sending me to Uganda… a country I'd never before set foot in.

33

THE LANDING

JAMBO!
(Hello in Swahili)

Wednesday, March 20, 2013

I arrived in Uganda for the first time on March 20, 2013. There's a fair bit that goes without saying for people who have visited an impoverished country. Monkeys aren't climbing the concrete stairs of most international airports; but they are at Entebbe, Uganda.

You can almost see the word bubble above the first-time visitor's head... "ohhhh-kay... soooooo... I'm in Africa-Africa."

Gazelle in headlights.

The first thing you realize is that your senses have been overwhelmed long before your brain realizes they've been overwhelmed.

Pictures can only prepare you so much. Your eyes can only take in so many new images into your brain until the 'blue-screen-of-death' takes hold inside your head. Your other senses have no mental receptors to attach to -- the way they do when you catch a whiff of the perfume that reminds you of the girl you dated in high school or touch a grapefruit and it reminds you of grandma's house all those summers ago. All the new sensory 'molecules' or whatever have nothing to attach to.

So you find yourself doing one of two things: Bringing out your camera to take a picture of every living thing or rummaging through your luggage for an Ambien so you can give your brain a rest. I honestly don't know if it's that everything is as dramatic as you think it is at the time, or the fact that you have been travelling on a plane for a *minimum* of eighteen hours straight and you are just maxed out from the journey. Maybe it's a combination of both?

From having read Katie's book and having spoken with Loren, I expected a smell much more dramatic than what I encountered as I stepped off the KLM airplane. Throughout the first week I was in Uganda, and just by nature, being a fairly observant person, I'm relatively certain I know what the smell is. In the U.S., many of us know the difference between the smell of someone burning pine versus oak in a campfire. The two different varieties of wood give off vastly different odors when burned. Uganda is the same; only it has completely different types of trees/wood, which in turn gives off a very different odor(s). Most of the wood that is burned is used for cooking. Because there is so much poverty in Uganda, people are burning fires constantly to get rid of their trash and to prepare food like rice, posho, beans, etc. So the smell is everywhere all the time. It's not a bad smell per-say; it's just not like anything else you've ever smelled before in the States.

We pulled away from the airport in Entebbe and I noticed there were stacks upon stacks of cargo shipping containers/pods inside a razor-wired fence the length of a couple football fields. They all said

"UN" on them. I asked the driver where all those went -- where the UN distributed them to?

The driver shrugged.

Having driven around the country, I'd have to say the same. In defense of the UN though, I don't think the issues I've seen in Uganda would be fixed with one hundred billion dollars in aid. The issues are too deep, too pervasive, and too long-standing.

I have to laugh a little.

The irony and reality is that Jesus encountered the exact same thing. He couldn't have 'fixed' the world with all the wealth and money in the Roman and Egyptian empires combined. The core problem He came to address was the sinfulness and depravity of the human soul. He used His two hands and two feet for three years... and then let them be nailed to a cross while gravity tugged at his body's weight against those very nails until 'it was finished'. He invested His life, those three years, into twelve completely ordinary men -- and changed the world forever.

Legislators throughout the world would do well to spend a little less time trying to build a fence of laws that constrain and a little more time addressing the question, "Why is everyone trying to get out of the fence we're trying to build for them?"

Spoiler alert: because we -- all of us -- are sinners.

We like being the King of our castle -- and we don't want anyone telling us where our fence (or moat) should or shouldn't be.

"I'll dig my moat where I darn well please, thank you very much!"

That's what the Bible identifies as the sinful nature and, at its core, is something called 'pride'. Sorry, it just is what it is. You and I have only one way to combat it that will cure the disease. The cure is a person, who chose to suffer beyond imagination and remove Hell from our life's deck of cards. See John 3:17 and 1 Thessalonians 5:9 if you think Jesus came to send everyone to Hell that didn't believe in Him. We condemn ourselves to Hell; that's why Jesus is called the Rescuer/Redeemer and not the Warden.

He is now wearing a robe of light. That makes putting chrome on our stuff look pretty ridiculous, no? I can't wait for Heaven!

34

WHAT I'VE LEARNED...
THUS FAR

Friday, April 5, 2013 (last day of maiden voyage to Uganda)

One of the questions I've been addressing in my journey to Uganda is a pretty basic one; "What am I supposed to learn here... or what have I learned?"

I've learned that 'sanitary' is a relative term.

I've learned that many of the worst roads in the USA are better than the best roads in Uganda.

I've learned speed bumps come in multiples of two in Uganda and it is entirely dependent on your driver whether or not you slow down for them. They are also, unfortunately, the most well-constructed things in the entire country.

I've learned there is a kid named Boo that is entertainment gold.

I've learned traffic laws are traffic-shlaws in Uganda.

I've learned there's a good reason every car has a metal brush-guard on the front; you're gonna need it.

I've learned that there are the exact same issues at the root of the problems in the USA as in Uganda. We in the States just tend to have more stuff to distract us, but the 'human-condition' remains a carbon-copy.

I've learned that a luke-warm church is not an American problem; it's a heart and Holy Spirit problem.

I've learned that worship isn't a cultural shape-shifter -- it's a Spirit thing that a church either has or does not have.

I've learned that there are people in all cultures that just want a hand-out; and there are people in all cultures that truly need a hand-up.

I've learned that baboons in Uganda are just as hesitant and schizophrenic when crossing the road as deer or squirrels are in the States.

I've learned that joy does not depend on whether or not your walls are made out of mud and sticks, or whether or not you've ever owned a pair of shoes, but on who resides as King of your heart.

I've learned that all children cry, smile, and belly-laugh in the same language.

I've learned that there are children in Uganda who have never seen arm hair or sunburned skin change color simply by pressing on it -- and that those things are more entertaining to them than all the video games in the world.

I've learned that sponsoring children through organizations like Helping Hands Foreign Missions, World Vision, Compassion International, etc. literally has the power to change the trajectory of a child's life and future for generations to come. I have witnessed this with my own eyes.

I've learned that Mzungu is a name that makes me smile.

I've learned that surrender is the wisest thing I can do each day.

I've learned that my two little hands and feet are the same instruments Jesus used to change the world.

I've learned that there are children in Africa who would be overjoyed to sleep on the mat in my bathroom. It beats the heck out of dirt.

I've learned that your world -- your whole life -- can change in a five minute conversation in a tiny little mission house kitchen half-way across the planet -- because our God *never* sleeps.

And I've learned the secret handshake in Uganda.

There's no secret in this story. It's really simple actually... it's just not easy. It wasn't easy for me at least. The Gospel is so simple a child can understand it and yet so difficult, a well-educated, full-grown adult will choose not do it. So what's the secret?

He bids me come and die -- and find that in that voluntary death, I will truly live. Lose your life in Jesus and you too will find a life beyond imagination... a life you've been wondering, "is it really possible -- does it really exist -- is it really available to *me*?"

> "I have been crucified with Christ and I no longer live, but Christ lives in, and, by the Holy Spirit, through me. The life I live in this body... in this one life I have, I live by faith in the Son of God... the Commander of the Armies of Heaven... the same One demons tremble at the very sound of His Name... who *LEFT HEAVEN*... for me(?!?!)... to be mocked, misunderstood, misrepresented, beaten, conspired against, whipped, spit on, abandoned, betrayed, tortured, speared, and murdered... while completely innocent... all so I could live this life as an imperfect reflection of a love that this physical world has never known but so desperately longs for".
> - Galatians 2:20 (my revised version)

And this is where I thought the 'book/chronicle' was
initially supposed to end... at least for a while.
God had other plans.

35

8,000 MILES FOR A
15-MINUTE DRIVE

Saturday, April 27, 2013

While I was in Uganda, the things I thought would be the biggest struggles/challenges -- like having to brush my teeth with bottled water, the complete lack of hot water, the poverty and trash everywhere -- well, they really weren't all that challenging. I don't know... I guess I had mentally prepared myself to adjust to these things fairly well? The thing that totally caught me off guard was this: In the depths of me, I hold such a strong desire to have a family of my own -- a loving and faithful wife to grow old with.

I came to the wall of realization about three or four days into the trip that, for these things to happen, God would be the only One who could bring about the fruition of these desires of my heart. At this point in the story, you might be thinking that I have some sort of 'bionic faith'. I don't. To quote Pinocchio, "I'm a real boy".

For the first several days of the trip, I found myself feeling like part of me was unengaged -- or maybe 'retracted' is a better way of saying it. While I was consciously and subconsciously going through this 'family-wife-life' reality, life in Uganda was still happening all around me.

My thought was basically this: "How on earth is God -- could God -- bring this to fruition? Yeah, He did and is doing it with me, but for this to happen *twice*?! For God to bring some other person through something like this, well, I don't want to say 'God can't', but I mean really!"

About six days into the trip, I found myself lying down, by myself, on the bed in the room I was staying in. My roommate for the two plus weeks I was in Uganda was more of a night owl, so he hadn't gotten in to turn down the sheets on the Nile Foam mattress, which is the standard issue in Uganda. The Nile Foam material is surprisingly comfortable considering the third world environment we were experiencing; it is somewhere between packaging foam and a memory foam bedding material. For what I was expecting, it was actually pretty comfortable.

I was lying on my side having a pretty hard conversation with God. I got to one point in the interchange at which point I had tears rolling down the bridge of my nose and falling onto the fitted sheet covering the foam mattress.

Without going into every detail, I just simply felt like God was telling me He knew the desires of my heart: the family, the wife -- and it was time I stop holding on to them and lay them down at His feet. It was as though these two things were the things I still treasured in my hear -- they were and are my dreams -- and God was very clearly saying, "I want you to delight yourself in Me, knowing that I know the desires of your heart and knowing that I care for you... but I want you to lay them down."

I came to the realization that Psalm 37:4, which I talked about earlier, "Delight yourself in the Lord and He will give you the desires of your heart" has a couple catches in it.

First, the receiving of the desires of my heart *follows* me delighting myself in the Lord.

Second... given the first... as I delight myself in the Lord, my hearts desires may actually change.

Third, there's no "if" anywhere in that verse.

God doesn't owe me a thing.

The tears that were rolling off my nose that night were -- very simply stated -- because I was afraid. I knew what God was telling me:

lay down the desires of my heart. My fear -- my one huge fear I referred to towards the end of Chapter 31 -- was that He would not pick them up. Like I've said, I'm a real person with real fears and a very real God.

The hardest part in the whole interchange was this: I knew I had to be ok with laying these things down because, as I've already said, I know He cares for me and He is not indebted to me to carry out some sort of 'cosmic favor' to make my life "happy".

I simply felt like the question was postured to my soul:
"Do... you... trust... Me?"
Yes.
"Enough to lay down your dreams?"
[deep sigh]... Yes.

The next day I felt more engaged into the surroundings, the people, and the tasks at hand for the day. I still mentally struggled with the surrender deal from the night before, but knew that the transaction within my will had taken place -- that I trusted God to care for me and ultimately do what was best for me. I had replayed so much of what had brought me to Uganda in the first place and realized, in light of this, the whole surrender of my dreams that I was being 'called out' on was, in reality, the most logical and sensible thing to do. Easy? Nope. But I knew it was best.

As each day went on, I felt lighter -- more joyful -- more at peace. By the end of the second week, oddly -- surprisingly, weirdly, I felt ok with the surrendering of my dreams. As I thought about it, I'd just shrug my shoulders and laugh to myself, "Dude... you're in stinkin' Uganda?! Look at all that God's done to place your butt in east Africa -- in a country you knew nothing of a year ago. He knows what He's doing -- you don't -- so let Him."

God's sovereignty -- His ability to make all things coalesce and redeem the garbage in our lives in the most unlikely of ways/methods -- is, frankly, one of the attributes of God that has the ability to regularly astound and befuddle me. As much, or even more so than 'the miraculous', is my amazement of how on earth God does what He does with the marginal, the woeful, and the horrendous content in our lives.

The day before we were scheduled to depart from Entebbe, Uganda and head back to Atlanta, GA, I was in the kitchen of the mission house we were staying in. We were very blessed to have electricity in the missions house, so there was a refrigerator, two mismatching wooden tables that were used to set food out on during meal times, and an old wooden bookcase that houses miscellaneous 'leftovers' from missions teams that had recently stayed at the property. I learned quickly that the hot sauce packets were what everyone was digging for in the condiment bucket. The walls of the kitchen were a faded beige plaster and the floor was painted a burnt terra-cotta-colored concrete. The contents of the refrigerator were usually just a few kinds of sodas and not much else since the power goes out all the time.

We had gotten back a little while earlier from our work for the day and I had just stepped into the kitchen to grab a Coke out of the fridge. Yes, they have Coke in the far reaches of the globe, and yes, it tastes better because there are only five ingredients in it (one of which is real cane sugar).

While I was removing the cap from the glass bottle, Trey walks in. This is the same Trey from back in November -- the person who I was connected with from Cliff, who Scott had connected me with after I had received Perry Nobles *Unleash!* book out of the blue at a house I had lived at for four months eight years ago. The same Trey who had then connected me with his father, Loren, in December and whom I had just flown 8,000miles on an airplane with about 17 days ago.

That Trey.

We start chit-chatting about the week for a few minutes, just kind of decompressing and analyzing a few things. As I think we're wrapping up the short conversation, Trey says, "So hey, when we get back to Georgia, Sarah (his wife) has one of her friends she wants to set you up with."

To say I was caught off guard is putting it mildly. I just about shot Coke fizz through my nose. I thanked him for the thought, but said I wasn't really wanting to or looking to date right now. I had enough stuff going on -- the thought of *more* emotional stuff in life was honestly a bit comical. I had already told two other people "No thanks" that were trying to set me up -- I just was not interested in further complicating this season of life -- whatever 'this season' turned out to be.

So I just told him I'd think about it, not really wanting to be rude, but also knowing I was more than likely just going to give him a polite, "Thanks, but no thanks" response when we got back to Georgia. The two things I shared with him that were huge "no-compromise" deals for me, if and when I did start dating, were these: 1. She has to be a 'whole' person -- sound and secure in both herself and her place in life, and 2. Her relationship and walk with Christ has to be visible -- tangible. Not an "I believe the same things you believe" faith, but a faith and relationship with Christ that is *easy* to see, both up close and at a distance.

Honestly, I realize from both the male and female perspectives, this is a tiny percentage of the population. And that was just my "pre-screening" starting block. The primary reason for these two is pretty simple; there are no perfect people. The first — the 'wholeness' of the individual -- simply gives a sound basis to start from and build a relationship on. The second -- the 'visibility' of their walk with Christ -- is really just because we all get thrown around from the events of life. If Jesus is not visible as the 'Calmer of the waves' in singleness, married life is going to be an absolute squall.

We touched down back at Hartsfield-Jackson International in Atlanta on April 6th.

On April 18th, Trey and I met up for lunch at La Parilla -- the first place I had met with his dad about a month after Trey and I initially connected.

I had been thinking and praying through the whole "being set up" deal in the interim. Having never been set up before, I was skeptical and felt more than a little uncomfortable. I figured Trey and I would just have lunch and talk; if he brought it up, we'd discuss it a little more, but I was not going to bring it up. So we went through about half of our lunch, when Trey looks across the table at me and says, "Sooo -- have you thought any more about what we talked about in the kitchen? Sarah's friend?"

Now mind you, I know nothing of this person. I'd never seen a picture, don't know any life facts -- don't even know a first name -- just that she's one of Sarah's good friends.

I responded, "You know, I really want to tell you 'no thanks', but in the process of my mental evaluation, I thought, 'of all the people I know and trust, who demonstrates my two 'no-compromise' aspects *themselves*? After all, if I'm being set up by someone who is not a whole person and doesn't have a tangible, visible relationship with Christ, what hope could I have that this mystery woman would have them?" But Trey and Sarah are on that short list -- a very short list. You can't be around them and not see Jesus. You can't help but be encouraged by being around them -- because whole people impart wholeness.

So I told Trey that the only reason -- the *only reason*, I would consider it was because of my confidence in his and Sarah's discernment based on their lives with Christ. Note: I still didn't say "yes". I just told him I'd continue thinking and praying about it.

Trey shared with me a quick thirty second life summary about this person, Amber. My first comment to him was, "Hmmm, I like that name!" Then he pulled up one of her pictures on his phone. The first picture he showed me of her looked like she might be a hair shampoo model. I tried to mask my "wowzers!" face and just looked at Trey and said, "Uhh, why do you have that picture on your phone dude?!" He said it was her Facebook page. We laughed, but for reals.

So we left lunch and I told him I'd keep thinking about it and walked out to my car in the parking lot, still processing all of this. Two days later, Saturday, I sent Sarah a message through Facebook and asked her opinion on something.

Evidently Amber and I were already both signed up to run a 5K in support of raising money for the building of an orphanage at the Village of Eden. I asked Sarah if she thought it was weird for me to 'friend request' Amber on Facebook. I didn't know at that point if Amber knew anything about me or knew Trey and Sarah were "scheming". [I later found out she had already Facebook stalked me – haha, c'mon people -- if you have a Facebook account, you have stalked someone too].

My only thought was to hopefully get through some of the initial awkwardness with meeting for the first time at a 5K and didn't know which situation would be less awkward/weird. I'm still not sure if this was a plus or minus on 'style points' for me with Sarah.

Sarah responded and told me to "go for it". So I sent Amber a 'friend request' around noon that Saturday. She accepted my 'friend request' later that afternoon. The first thing she told me was that the only reason she agreed to be set up was because she trusted Trey and Sarah to look past the physical and discern the other persons character, their walk with Christ, and their wholeness as a person -- basically the exact same reason -- *the only reason* I said 'yes' as well.

In our first conversation that night, she told me that one of her life dreams was to be a missionary -- knowing nothing of my story, only that I had been to Uganda with Trey and Sarah. I still remember how my jaw literally fell open when she said that -- and that she would have no problem living off rice and beans. We chatted for almost two hours that night.

This is my journal entry from that evening:

4/21/13 1:19am

> I just had an 1½ hour conversation with the woman I'm going to spend the rest of my life with, Amber Allen. God, I have no earthly idea where to begin or end. I just feel like You are already looking at this night and saying "I told you so!" This woman is almost a clone of me... the no TV service, the running/exercising, the 4:30am early riser, the marketing degree, the sense of humor, and You... most of all... You Jesus. She has You and You have her. I've never looked forward to meeting someone as much as this in my entire life. This doesn't even feel real. Jesus, give me all the wisdom and follow through I need to lead this daughter of Yours into a deeper relationship with You and a greater love for herself and others. Strengthen me to be the man You call me to be.

Amber and I talked the next few days and continued to discover just how eerily similar we were to each other -- it was both comical and incredible.

We met for the very first time four days later over our lunch break at Elachee Nature Center, which is towards the south end of Gainesville. That was Thursday, April 25, 2013.

The very next day, Friday, April 26th, we met again over lunch. We went for a walk on one of the nearby trails. I picked her up off the ground and placed her feet on a log about six inch off the ground and she began sharing some stuff from her day with me. I stood there and had this mental conversation in my head…

"You know you know, why don't you just tell her".

"I can't tell her -- that's, well, it's just nuts".

"Yeah, but you know she's already there with you -- so just say it".

"Nah, I can't say that -- that's ridiculous".

"Yeah, but it's the same thing she's thinking and so you're both ridiculous".

This kind of internal conversation went on for a couple minutes.

Sometimes it's exhausting being inside my head.

So I eventually looked down at the ground, took a deep breath as I shook my head in absolute disbelief at what was about to come out of my mouth, looked up, met her eyes, and said, "Amber, I have no idea how, but somehow I know I'm going to spend the rest of my life with you".

She didn't freeze.

She didn't break out into a cold sweat.

She didn't take off running.

She didn't say "What?!" and slap me in the face.

She jumped off the log, grabbed onto my neck, and said the same thing to me.

How on earth does this happen?

It would appear -- delighting yourself in the Lord.

Trusting that He cares for you.

Living out the reality that He, not me, knows what is best for my life. Why has this happened *to me*? I have no idea. I certainly don't deserve it and I personally know people who are much better examples of what it looks like to delight in the Lord that are still waiting for the floodgates to open. I don't know how this works, I just know that our God works all things for the good of those who love Him and are called according to His purpose. Am I glad this was part of God's purpose? You bet'cha. But it's not a one-sided deal.

The thing is, Amber was at the same place God had brought me to -- not looking to date -- laying down the desires of her heart. A single mom of two great boys with a full-time job, she had resigned herself to "this is going to be my life... two great children... a job that makes ends meet... a good church... God doesn't owe me anything". God had the desires of her heart in one of His proverbial hands. I'm thinking He was just waiting on me to put the desires of my heart in His other hand, so that then and only then, could He freely bring them both together in a fashion that truly had His fingerprints all over it.

Several people who have tracked with me through this story have commented that they wish they had my 'great faith'.

They couldn't be further from the truth.

Everything over the course of this story -- the chronicle that has unfolded thus far -- is one small step of obedience... followed by one small step of obedience... followed by one small step of obedience.

That's... about... it.

Did I make mistakes through the process? Your better believe it! But those small steps of obedience took me 8,000 miles from my home, which was the only place -- the only way I could have met the woman of my dreams -- who lives a short fifteen minute drive from my front door in Georgia. I would have never met her if I hadn't been in that mission house kitchen in Busia, Uganda on April 4, 2013. There is no life, social, or professional circle that would have otherwise brought us together.

The 'made in Heaven' match wasn't hard to see by others either, which is why Trey married us a few weeks later.

Some people nearly pass-out when they hear this -- or they sit there inwardly biting their fingernails like "oh I hope he didn't go off the deep-end". So let me share with you just one of the things I couldn't get out of my head these first few weeks.

Jesus gave a lot of parables, or illustrative stories, in His communication throughout the Gospels. One of them -- one of the shortest ones -- I couldn't stop thinking about. It's Jesus literally communicating a critical aspect of discovering His homeland -- the Kingdom of Heaven, by using only one verse.

> "The kingdom of heaven is like treasure hidden in a field. When a man found it, he hid it again, and then in his joy went and sold all he had and bought that field." Matthew 13:44(NIV)

So while it is certainly not advisable for every couple to get married after only a few weeks of knowing each other (especially when children are involved), and while I know how I would counsel someone in a similar situation -- I can't explain this thing with Amber, nor can she. We just knew that we knew that we knew before we ever saw each other.

My central thought those first few weeks was simple; I had found one of God's treasures 'buried in a field'. If you were walking through a cow pasture and tripped over a gold nugget the size of an automobile, would you care what people thought when you sold whatever was necessary to buy that field? In fifty years, people won't think it's so crazy, just like the guy who sold his life away to buy a random field on the outskirts of town, when everyone thought he went nuts. It was only a short while later he had the wealth to buy the entire town.

One of the kids said to her after the first time we had dinner together, "I know you and Jake haven't known each other that long, but it seems like you've known each other for years". And that's exactly how it felt for both of us from the very first conversation. The only thing that has been weird in the whole mix of things is that nothing has felt weird. I realize that sounds bizarre, but all the things that should feel weird from a 'blended family' perspective couldn't have felt more natural for all parties involved.

I used to wonder what people were thinking when I'd hear them say things like "when you know, you know".

I used to roll my eyes a little while sitting in Sunday school classes or Bible studies when I'd hear people say things like "All you need to do is focus on growing closer to God and He will bring someone alongside you that is doing the same thing."

Yeah, that's why eHarmony and Match.com exist right?

Welp... now I'm going to be 'that guy'.

The third and last song I'll share is one I came across the first week in May. There are some songs in life that become "someone's song" -- the song that every time you hear it on the radio, you effortlessly, instantly teleport to somewhere -- with someone. The song "Sovereign" by Chris Tomlin is the third song. Every time I hear it, I teleport into a tiny mission house kitchen just off an unmarked, deeply rutted, and altogether unsuspecting dirt road in a little village known as Busia, Uganda.

There are clothes hanging up on a few drooping clotheslines, drying yet again from being rinsed a second time by the afternoon showers. It's the rainy season.

High school students are playing the card game Dutch Blitz on an old picnic table situated on top of the red concrete slab to my right.

Boo is walking around without any pants on -- again. He hasn't had any pants on all day I don't think.

I'm wearing one of three shirts I wore on the trip and the same pair of breathable pants. I'm pretty sure I smell horrendous.

I'm removing the red cap of a glass Coke bottle while I lean up against the door frame and talk to a friend named Trey, who catches me totally off guard with one question.

I have no clue my life is about to change forever.

This is a song about Jesus, but this will forever remind me of Amber.

I can honestly say...

```
"In your everlasting arms
All the pieces of my life
From beginning to the end
    I can trust you"
```

36

A STINKIN' POND

Friday, June 14, 2013

After God had orchestrated the selling of my house in February, I continually prayed through the question of "so what am I supposed to do with all the proceeds from the sale?" It wasn't a fortune, but it was more money than I'd ever had in my savings account before.

Before I launch into the rest of this chapter, I think it is probably pertinent to explain one thing: this money was entirely surrendered to God. I mean, I would constantly be in prayer throughout my day at work, while I was out jogging -- wherever, whenever -- I was so incredibly nervous about doing the wrong thing with this money God had sent my way, especially given the events leading up to the selling of the house. I was literally prepared to give it all away to fund the missions work in Uganda or to invest it in whatever else God wanted -- I just wasn't certain I knew what He wanted me to do with it.

While I was in Uganda with Loren, a thought hit me. It was a thought I hadn't considered before. You might think the thought would be how the money could be used to build a school, or houses, or buy clothes, or provide food. While all those things are good and needed, that wasn't what hit me. The thought was this: Loren does what he does now as a missionary because when his father-in-law passed away, he had left the family enough money to pay off their mortgage, giving him financial freedom to serve as a missionary. So the thought that I began praying through was this: what if I could find a house that I could pay off in a short period of time that could not only be debt-free place to return to while back state-side from Uganda, but also be a potential source of revenue (which missionaries desperately need). What if I could find a house with an unfinished basement that I could convert to be an apartment or 'mother-in-law suite' that I could then rent out and not only have no debt on the house, but have it be a source of income to help support my time in Uganda?

So when I got back from Uganda, I began looking with my real estate agent for a house in our same county with either a basement that I could remodel to make an apartment, or a place that had enough property to build a small above-the-garage suite on. Having built the house I sold in February, I had a pretty good grasp on the cost, so we began looking. CJ made a comment to me when we started the process. "You know Jake," she said, "I think God is going to make it painfully obvious where He wants you given all the stuff that's happened. I don't think you're going to have a lot of guess work with this as far as the house goes."

Week after week after week -- the same story. She'd email me some new listings. I'd look at them and email her back saying "Can we look at the one on X-street and Y-circle this week?" She would email me back, "They both went under contract yesterday" -- "two days ago" -- "today" and so on. One of the homes we were literally standing in the home, having walked through it, when she got a text message back from the listing agent that said, "Went under contract this morning".

We looked at a bunch of foreclosures that I thought had promise. Three of them I bid on. Of these three houses, two had streams on the property. It has been a dream of mine to someday have a house that had a stream on the property; its part of the kid inside me that will never grow up/old.

The three foreclosures all had a ten-day preview period in which prospective buyers are able to look at and walk through the houses. After looking at them, I waited until the last twenty-four hours to submit my bid.

The first house had thirteen other bids in when I put mine in. Didn't get it.

The second house had three other bids when I put mine in. Didn't get it.

The third house only had one other bid. I figured it was a low-ball offer most likely. I asked CJ what she thought a solid bid amount would be given the last two strikeouts. She told me a bid price that sounded reasonable. I went about three percent over that number. On Monday, June 10th, I was supposed to hear back on the bid. Third time's a charm right? Nope. Lost again.

The next day Trey and I met up for lunch. Since the trip to Uganda, I had this weird feeling -- the same type of sensation I had from back in the Fall of "what is about to happen" from somewhere within me -- the feeling that he and I were going to be involved in ministry together somehow. I figured it would be centered around Uganda and the Village of Eden, but it seemed a little deeper than that. Amber and I were committed to serving at her church because she was on staff there, so I didn't figure there could really be a whole lot of crossover beyond trips to Uganda.

Over lunch, I shared with Trey the latest with the house stuff. My comment to him that day was this: "I know closed doors are just as much an answer to prayer as open doors, but my forehead is getting worn out by doors hitting me in the face." We went on to talk about some other ministry stuff and concluded our conversation somehow by talking about Amber's job. I have no idea how we got on this subject.

Amber is on staff at her church, with a job function and skill set that is transferable beyond the church sphere. Trey asked if she would ever think about working outside the church -- if she wanted to stay in a church environment, or if it mattered to her. It was comical to me because Amber and I had been out running together a few days earlier and were discussing some work stuff and that very topic had come up during our conversation.

I told Trey that based on our conversation I didn't think there was a strong preference either way, but that if the right thing came along at the right time, she and I would talk it over and pray about it. But we were content where we were at right now.

The next day, Trey calls me around 4:00pm. I see him on my caller ID, so I grab the cell phone off my office desk and walk down the hallway into our conference room. This is how our conversation goes:

Me: "Hey man, what's up?"

Trey: "So look -- I don't know what it is with you and 'speaking things into being' or whatever, but our Administrative Pastor just left my office. He came in to tell me that our bookkeeper of eight years had come in to his office this morning and turned in her resignation -- she's moving back to Arizona to be closer to her kids and grandkids. It was completely unannounced. He came in the tell me and ask if I knew anyone that might be a good fit for the job?"

Me: "Shut your face! You've got to be kidding me?!"

Trey: [laughing] "Dude, I don't know what to tell you and I don't want to sway you off whatever path God has you both on, but if you and Amber think this might be what God's leading you to, send me her resume and I'll pass it along".

Me: "Umm, yeah -- we will talk about it tonight."

We hung up and I walked down the hallway to my office thinking to myself, "What on earth God?! The next day?? Really?? Good grief, what next?!"

Amber and I talked it over on our run that evening. The job situation was a big step. We were excited about the possibility of a job change that would enable us to engage in ministry with Trey and Sarah, so we agreed to at least get Amber's name in the hat.

After we finished our run, we cleaned up and sat down to have dinner and talk over some things a little more. While there was some excitement about the job situation, I was feeling extremely discouraged about the house search. Amber's house was for sale and with it being in a popular area and a good school district, we felt the house would sell over the summer moving/selling season -- so the time was counting down to find a 'new' home. My criteria hadn't changed from before; I still felt like the thing I was supposed to do was find the house with the unfinished basement, get it paid off as quickly as possible, and get over to Uganda. God had brought me a wife with the same heart, I think because He knows "two are better than one because they have a better return on their labor" (Ecclesiastes 4:9 NIV).

Now we take a short rabbit trail off the story line of our dinner discussion with the house to my quiet time that same morning. Just keep in mind the order of events:

Tuesday: Lunch with Trey.

Wednesday morning: The quiet time I'm about to share.

Wednesday lunchtime: A staff lunch planned by our Office Manager, Kelly.

Wednesday afternoon 4:00pm: The call from Trey about job.

Wednesday night: I will return to this place after I tell you about the quiet time.

As we woke up Wednesday morning and mulled around the kitchen, I remembered I didn't need to plan for lunch. We had a staff lunch today and I had a plan. Our company manages a property that has a very small laundry facility on it. It's not a moneymaker by any stretch of the imagination, but over the last couple months, we had collected a little bit of change from it. The property is a low-end foreclosure and the asset manager we deal with for the bank is without a doubt one of the most unreasonable and unnecessarily difficult people anyone in our company has ever had to deal with. So difficult, that we have made a collective internal decision to never work with this person again on any business deals, no matter the price tag. It's *that* bad. Everyone going on the lunch has, in some fashion, had to work with this asset manager and has felt "the pain".

The thought I had -- the motive of my heart -- was to use the money (or at least some of it) we had collected from the laundry machines, to buy lunch for the staff -- just as a "thank you for hanging in there" type thing. We were going to a local restaurant and the collective bill would probably be less than sixty dollars, so no big deal right? Whelp, the thing about it was/is this: it was simply not my/our money to spend. It belonged to the property -- to the asset manager from Hades.

Every time I thought about it, I felt God convicting me of the same thing again and again and again, "Son, I call this stealing -- quit trying to call it something else -- it's also called 'sin' in case you were wondering". These thoughts ran through my mind while I sat down at the kitchen table to have my quiet time.

I'm sharing this for two reasons. First, so no one reading this thinks I am any better, more holy, or whatever you want to call it, than anyone else. The Christian life is a life of being purified by a Holy God and I have a lot of stuff that still needs to be worked on as you can see. The apostle Paul refers to it as "working out your salvation" in Philippians 2:12. I recognize that you almost never hear pastors talk about their own personal sin from the pulpit/stage, which I think leads people to the assumption that they have a better, more 'holy' grasp on life's challenges. Sometimes that may very well be the case, but it can also create this elevated and unapproachable rift between the pastor and the people, which I think must be both comical and saddening to God. See Romans 3:23 if you are persuaded otherwise.

The second reason I share this is because of what God can do with our responses to this sort of conviction, as you are about to read.

In my reading that morning, I was continuing through the second half of Psalm 18. I began reading where I had left off the day before, in verse 16.

16 He reached down from on high and took hold of me;
    He drew me out of deep waters.
17 He rescued me from my powerful enemy, from my foes,
    who were too strong for me.

¹⁸ They confronted me in the day of my disaster, but
the Lᴏʀᴅ was my support.
¹⁹ He brought me out into a spacious place; He rescued
me because He delighted in me. (NIV)

My mind briefly flipped through the mental scrapbook of all that God had done and was continuing to do since last August.

"Yep, I know exactly what David is talking about here. I know what it feels like to have the hand of God reach down and take hold of you and draw you out of the deep -- to be my Support and Rescuer -- and it's simply because He delighted in me. Such a good passage!" I thought, as I continued to verse 20, at which point God got His metaphorical chess board out and plopped it down on top of my Bible.

I've italicized a few parts on this next passage as a small means of showing the emphasis that the Holy Spirit hit me upside the head with as I continued reading Psalm 18. Feel free to laugh at me as you read.

²⁰ The Lᴏʀᴅ has dealt with *me* according to *my*
righteousness; according to *the cleanness of my
hands* He has rewarded me.
²¹ For I have kept the ways of the Lᴏʀᴅ;
I am not guilty of turning from my God.
²² *All* His laws are before me;
I have not turned away from His decrees.
²³ I have been *blameless* before Him
and have *kept myself from sin.*
²⁴ The Lᴏʀᴅ has rewarded me according to my righteousness,
according to the cleanness of my hands *in His sight.*
²⁵ To the faithful You show Yourself faithful,
to the blameless You show Yourself blameless,
²⁶ to the pure You show Yourself pure,
but to the devious You show Yourself shrewd.
²⁷ You save the humble
but bring low those whose eyes are haughty.
²⁸ You, Lᴏʀᴅ, keep my lamp burning;
my God turns my darkness into light.
²⁹ With Your help I can advance against a troop;
with my God I can scale a wall.
³⁰ As for God, *His way is perfect*:
The Lᴏʀᴅ's word is flawless;

He shields all who take refuge in Him. (NIV)

Checkmate.

I sat there and laughed, rolled my eyes a little, and took my whooping; resigning myself to the fact that the intentions and motives within me were the devious workings of sin I had been plotting out.

I stopped at Lowes on the way to work that morning and took the 'lunch money' and got a gift card for our maintenance staff to use for supplies for the property, so that the money from the property was used for the property.

The staff lunch went as planned; individual checks.

Now we return to the dinner conversation, which occurs three or four hours after the phone call from Trey about the job. Amber and I are sitting at the dinner table talking about the job situation. She can tell I'm bothered about the house search as well.

Since returning from Uganda, I had probably seriously looked at around twenty or thirty houses; every one of them I had gotten stonewalled almost immediately, as I mentioned earlier. I shared with Amber the same thing I had shared with Trey the day before... how I acknowledged that closed doors are an answer to prayer, but that I was getting a headache from so many doors hitting me in the forehead. Then I launched into this little tirade...

"I mean come on!" I sprang into my rant, "My lifelong dream of owning a home -- I mean not just a house, but the home you are going to live in for the majority of your life -- the dream I've always had was to have a house with a stream on the property. And there has not just been one, But *two* of the three foreclosures that had streams on the property! I mean *seriously*?! What are the odds of that?! And I got stymied on them both! Ok, thirteen bids, I'm ok with loosing out on that one, but against *one* other bid and I go over what CJ said... and *still* don't get it?!" I felt so deflated.

"I think the house we're supposed to have needs to have an unfinished basement (for the reasons I've already discussed), I want to find something in the kids school district". I paused with a degree of reservation and put my head down on my left forearm, which was resting on the kitchen table and spoke onto the surface of the table, "but my life dream, for whatever reason, is to have a stream." I paused for a half second and felt this short burst of frustration. I slammed my right fist down on the kitchen table, jolting the silverware off the plates to make a light clanging sound. "And dang-it, I want a pond *with* the stream!"

Amber took her left hand and rubbed the back of my head. "I think the house can't just be a normal thing -- I think with everything else that's happened, well -- I think it has to be 'book-worthy' you know," she said with a soft smile.

I then shared with her my quiet time from that morning and told her how I felt so convicted that I was asking God to do something, to work out something on my behalf, while I had been plotting out this sin in my heart. It frustrates me to no end, but it is a good reminder to me that I have not 'arrived' yet. I told her I felt like the intentions of my heart, which are never hidden from God, may have been part of the cause of all this frustration, which made me even more frustrated with myself. We talked some more, we prayed some more. The sun went down and the sun came up Thursday morning.

Thursday morning, Amber sends me an email. From the subject line, I can see it's a link to a Georgia MLS webpage. All she says in the body of the email is, "Just take a look. It's a little more than the price range we were looking, but it looks nice." I emailed her a quick response that I'd look at it later, to which she replies, "I can't tell what that dark thing is in middle -- behind the house. It looks like either an oil slick or a small body of water or something."

I froze at my desk.

I immediately pulled up the link.

I still remember staring at my laptop's screen and saying under my breath, "That... that's a stinkin' pond?!" I pulled up a website that shows bodies of water on it -- it wasn't just a pond -- it had a stream feeding the pond. And the house had an unfinished basement and was in the kid's school district right?

Check and check.

I went to look at it Friday morning with Amber and CJ, as all three of us were driving from different locations. I arrived at the house about fifteen minutes early. I walked down the hill to the pond and then up to the small field behind the pond. As I walked back up to the covered porch, Amber pulled in the driveway. She stepped out of her car and smiled at me. I took one look at her and, having not yet set foot inside the house said, "Welcome to your new home".

We went on to look through the house with CJ. Amber and I stayed in the driveway talking for a few minutes as CJ pulled out of the cul-de-sac. The conversation comes to a conclusion, or so I think, when Amber gets this big grin on her face.

I smiled back at her and said, "What?"

"It's *exciting* being married to you!!!" she blurts out as she gives me a hug and laughs.

We put an offer on the house that afternoon and went under contract two days later. The following week Amber was offered and accepted the job as part of the staff at Trey and Sarah's church. Our family is now getting settled into some new roles and environments at the church and loving the opportunities to serve.

Suffice to say…

30 As for God, *His way is perfect*:
The Lord's word is flawless;
He shields all who take refuge in Him.
(Psalm 18:30 NIV)

37

FAST & PRAY

Summer 2013

Over the course of the summer, we were able to spend some time as a family going to various 'things' involving the Village of Eden. I kept noticing how many occasions were piling up over a relatively short period of time for our new family to spend with people involved with the Village of Eden. It was kind of weird -- but good-weird.

Our first family event was on relatively short notice. We happened to get seats at one of the tables our church purchased at the annual gala for Helping Hands Foreign Missions. Several other church staffers were unable to attend so the four of us drove over to the conference facility on a rainy Saturday evening. The conference facility, located only about twenty minutes from our house, was bustling with people attending the gala by the time we arrived, fashionably late. To say the move-in process was taking its toll on me is putting it mildly. I truly needed this evening 'off'. We were about seventy-five percent of the way into doing some renovations to the kitchen and master bath, which, as it turns out, are relatively critical things in a house. You don't realize the value of things like countertops and sinks until 'they gone'.

It was a packed house at the gala and by the end of the night, I was very glad we had gone, for more than one reason. The first is, I got reunited with one of my most beloved candies: Mike & Ike's. I have little to no self-control with them, having brought sugar headaches upon myself on more than one occasion; they have almost always been directly related to the over consumption of Mike & Ike's. I don't buy them anymore because, well, do you have any idea how many Mike & Ike's you have to eat in a fifteen-minute time window to give yourself a sugar headache?

I have issues.

But they were on the table and there were seven other people at the table, so peer pressured self-control won out that night.

The gala was great because it gave Amber, Blake, and Chandler the opportunity to see, live and in person, the people I had been over to Uganda with. Some of the Ugandan's that our team had visited and grew to love had come over to visit as well, so it was a double bonus. As I mentioned, it gave my mind a respite from the woes of house moving and renovations, which I desperately needed. It also added another piece in this story.

Amber's passion, which she shared with me the first or second conversation we had, is to be involved in medical missions. In the first four conversations we had, she mentioned this and mentioned "Africa" two or three times. I still remember feeling my jaw drop wide open the first time she said something about "going to Africa". All she knew about me at that stage in our conversation was that I had been on a mission trip to Uganda with Trey and Sarah, not that I was headed over there on a longer term basis.

When I had gotten in touch with Loren last year, he told me what all they were building currently and that the next big project would be a ministry training facility for pastors in the region. There is almost no ministry training whatsoever, I later learned, so the local theology can be very incomplete and misinformed, for no other reason than some of the pastors have never had access to a basic commentary or study guide.

At the gala, Dr. Brenda Kowalski updated the crowd of several hundred supporters on the progress at the Village of Eden. Then she launched into the next big project at the property; the medical clinic. I watched Amber, over the next twenty minutes or so, steadily wipe tears away from her eyes and just kept thinking to myself as we listened, "ohhhh boy". It was something akin to the feeling you have as you ratchet up to the last few feet of a roller coaster before the first big plunge. You can't see over the hump, but you know something's coming as your stomach tightens and your neck tenses up.

Blake and Chandler are playing games with the Mike & Ike's, but Amber and I were both just sitting there trying to avoid passing out from the "Are you stinkin' kidding me?!" thoughts going through our heads.

In the ensuing weeks, we were able to have dinner a couple times with the Ugandans that were visiting before they headed home. We found out they are in love with Colonel Sanders Original Recipe, so we had some form of chicken with each of the dinners.

One morning, late into the summer, I was praying on the way to the gym and found myself in tears yet again, just asking God "How? How can all this that I see -- and feel -- and believe is happening... how?! How can this happen?" I knew I would need to start fundraising to fill the gap of a full or partial salary leaving the family income stream, but I had no idea how much I would need to raise, where it would come from, what my travel schedule would look like, and on and on my mind went in circles.

Yet as I drove and prayed, I felt a simple but overwhelming conviction that the Holy Spirit's response was very simply, "Jake... 'How' has *never* been your department. Your department is 'Yes' and 'Amen' *[The Biblical term 'amen' literally translates 'so be it'... in modern vernacular 'Ok God, I'm with You']*... that's it. If you get involved in the 'how', it's going to be messy." I immediately thought of Abram in Genesis 12 and how he got involved in the 'how'. Not the smartest move.

The following Sunday, Amber and I were in the car on the way to lunch with Trey and Sarah, talking about who knows what. I was feeling so burdened by all of this, I was silently praying as I drove and the three of them conversed. I remember exactly where we were... coming up to the overpass on Interstate 985, crossing over Exit 20. I was literally praying over the 'how' and of all this with the Village of Eden when Amber turns to me, thinking I was following whatever they were talking about, and says "Delayed obedience is the same thing as disobedience, isn't that right!" I smiled, took a deep breath, and nodded, "Yep".

I had told Amber while we were away on our honeymoon that I knew God brought us together for a reason and that I knew He was still wanting me involved in Uganda, I just had no idea how those two things intermix. We talked a couple hours about it on that afternoon in the Caribbean, me thinking the whole time, "This may be the last time I ever see clear blue water". She cried on the drive from the hotel to the little island airport. She later told me she was just overwhelmed with why she got to go somewhere like this? Why God had chosen to be so good to her? She said she wanted her life to be about something bigger than the American dream, but never thought she would get the opportunity that was unfolding before her eyes.

Then the week of September 9th hits. I had told Amber I felt like God was pulling me into a fast, so I was going to take a day to fast and pray this week, to try and gain some clarity and hear better from Him. I feel like I should say/qualify this, especially regarding Jesus comments on fasting in Matthew 6: I stink at this spiritual discipline. Like... it's embarrassing. I *really* don't want people thinking I'm trying to elevate myself in any way whatsoever. It is a struggle for me simply because I love food. Will-power over food throughout the course of my life looks something like the scoreboard of the original Dream Team (NBA Hall of Famers in the 1992 Olympics) and every other team they played -- *that* kind of embarrassing. So please, understand the reason for sharing this has everything to do with God's voice and absolutely nothing to do with my fasting; it's just part of the landscape of the story.

So I decided to fast on Wednesday. Over my lunch break, I got in my car and drove about two minutes from my office to a small park on the north side of Gainesville. It's a fairly popular place for people who are brown-bagging it for lunch to pull their car up to and have some 'me time' over their lunch break. It's just below some tennis courts and ball fields, so there's usually a fair bit of activity in the event the car radio isn't enough entertainment over lunch.

I parked the car, uttered a short, but very sincere prayer; something like "God, I... I just want to hear from You" and flopped open my Bible to a random place in the Old Testament. No bookmark, no leaflet. I just stuck my thumb in the OT and opened. The page was one I had been to several times over the years. It was David's prayer at the end of 1 Chronicles, beginning around chapter 29:10 and following. David says several times in several different ways, that everything he has comes from God and every material possession he has been given on Earth, comes from God, because they are His. "Ok God" I thought, "I know it's all Yours, it's just -- just kinda 'big-giant-yikes' for me at the moment. But I know where You guide, You provide." Then I flipped back a page (not forward, for some reason) and my eyes fixed on a verse I had highlighted at some point in the ten years I've owned this Bible. The verse is 1 Chronicles 28:10 and it's a fairly intimate and significant conversation between King David and his son Solomon regarding the future building of God's temple. For those who don't know, the temple construction was God's assigned task to be completed by Solomon. David leads into verse 10 by telling Solomon how important it is that Solomon keep God as the center of his devotion. Then in verse 10, David says,

> "Consider now, for the Lord has chosen you to build a temple as a sanctuary. Be strong and do the work." (NIV)

I sat there in my car and dropped my head with a big sigh, feeling like that was God's voice speaking into my life once again, "Jake, I have chosen you, because, as I spoke to you months ago, you will go. Now be strong and do the work I have given you to do."

I thought, as I drove back through the interconnecting stop signs leading back to the office, which would be harder: leaving for Africa, having the desires of my heart hanging in the balance, unfulfilled and solely dependent on God to move/act -- or having the longings and dreams of my heart fulfilled in spades and still being called to go. I really don't know which is harder, but I cycled back to a verse I had focused on during the first half of the year.

Acts 20:24.

The Apostle Paul is speaking to the early church and despite all his Jewish training and 'status' in the early church, he says this...

> "Nevertheless, I consider my life worth nothing to me, if only I may finish the race and complete the task the Lord Jesus has given me – the task of testifying to the gospel of God's grace." Acts 20:24 (NIV)

The question I would consistently posture to myself is this: "Do you consider your own life worth nothing in comparison to finishing the race, the task that God has given you to do?" It's a good exercise of the mind and the will for me personally, because when I stand before God to give an account of the one life He's given me, I have a feeling that's going to be a pretty important one to have nailed down. And over the last month or so, my mind kept getting drawn back to the account of Abram in Genesis 12. God called him to become a great nation and basically told him, "Get your immediate family, leave everything else you know, and go that'a'way. I'll tell you when you've gone far enough." Abram didn't do things perfectly, but his obedience demonstrates that at the end of the day, he counted his life as nothing for the sake of the call of God.

That evening we had a mid-week service at church for our middle school and high school students. I arrived a little early and sat at one of the back tables to spend some more time reading and processing. I was only in the church for about five minutes when Brandon, who works with Trey at the church, comes up to me and asks if I would help facilitate some of the discussion with the students after the middle school service. I said I would be glad to help. He then puts down on the table in front of me a piece of paper. It's a list of discussion questions to help guide the student through -- they all have to do with being on a mission from God -- and at the bottom of the page, in big blue letters, in a font made to look like hand-writing, it reads, "Now, why do you delay?"

Ha… ha… ha.

The students enter sporadically over the next fifteen to twenty minutes. Trey goes through the message he had prepared for the students, and talks about living life 'on mission' for Christ. As the students begin to file out of the room and go to their respective rooms for discussion, Trey holds up these little white business cards with something written on them and tells the students to all grab one on the way out. I wait to file in behind the students. I reach down and grab a couple in stride as I walk by.

I look down at what's in my right hand.

I roll my eyes and laugh to myself -- or at myself.

The cards read, "Why do you delay – Acts 20:24".

Yeah… really.

The actual card I picked up

You think I'm really "special" don't you?

Now I'm just waiting on the talking donkey to show up and ring my doorbell. See the Book of Numbers, Chapter 22 if you don't get that.

So that was Wednesday. On Sunday, Amber and I got in the car to go pick the kids up from the grandparents on the north side of Atlanta. The sermon at our church that morning had been about none other than Abram. Shocker, right? As we drove out of the neighborhood, I began to share with Amber all that had taken place that week and just said, "I don't know what this is going to look like -- I don't have a clue, but I know that God is still wanting me to help at the Village of Eden. I can't imagine being away from you and the kids for long, but I believe that is what's going to happen. I just don't know how, but I know 'how' is not a reason to not step out in faith." As Amber and I talked in the car, we identified a couple common things in almost all the Biblical accounts we read.

First, God gives clear instructions. Satan is the author of confusion, not Jesus.

Second, God never gives all the details you would like to have before saying 'yes'.

And third, God does not seem to align His plans, or assignments, with things that are "easy".

As we continued to converse, Amber tells me, through tears, that this morning, as she was walking through the church halls during the time I was in Sunday School with the 6th grade boys, she felt God telling her He was still sending me to the Village of Eden, but that He had opened the door -- the *one door* (her staff position with the church) months ago, because this was the church and the staff that would care for her and the boys while I was away.

Then she says, "I know that the wives (families) of our military soldiers sacrifice their 'family-time' all across the country every day to defend our country and keep us safe, and I just can't help but think to myself 'what greater sacrifice could I offer God than for us to support you in helping build a Village that will take Jesus to the families in Uganda?' I know it's going to be hard, but I'm with you."

She may be the greatest woman I've ever known.

38

OUR DAILY BREAD

Tuesday, September 16, 2013

One of the things Amber shared with me when we first met, when she was sharing with me that her heart was to be involved in missions work, was that her only real fear was of her kids going hungry. She said she knew and trusted Psalm 37:25, which reads…

> "I have been young, and now am old, yet I have not seen the righteous forsaken or his children begging for bread." (ESV)

Yet knowing that, she never thought she would have an opportunity to do any sort of missions work prior to the kids going off to college. Even then, it's still not easy.

The morning of September 16th, she sends me an email. The subject line reads "Seriously HE is so good…"

This is her email:

> So as I was running this morning I was asking God to make this dummy proof for me. I became more firm in trusting the fact that God is in control… remember one day I told you my fear in stepping out like this is not having food to feed our family but I trusted God's word and I quoted "never have I seen the righteous forsaken or his seed begging for bread…" Well on my way to the restroom I picked up a "Daily Bread" outside the office door and began to read today's entry as I walked (never have I done that). Well… the scripture is THAT very

one… and it clearly says what you have been saying in the devotion… OBEDIENCE is what God is after and He will take care of the rest. Ok I am starting to get it. And another thing… as I was running I kept having the overwhelming thought that YOU in my life are a tangible manifestation of God's love and faithfulness. Wow is all I can say today… OK I am getting back to work. ❤❤❤ oh how I love my husband!!

And here's the page from "Our Daily Bread". I think it's hysterical. I think they may have plagiarized some stuff from this book -- haha!

GOD'S WILL

READ:
Psalm 37:23-40

The steps of a good man are ordered by the LORD, and He delights in his way.
—Psalm 37:23

THE BIBLE IN ONE YEAR
Proverbs 25, 26
2 Corinthians 9

We're often looking for God's will—especially when we're in a difficult situation. We wonder, *What will happen to me here? Should I stay or does God want me somewhere else?* The only way to know for sure is to do what He asks you to do right now—the duty of the present moment—and wait for God to reveal the next step.

As you obey what you know, you will be strengthened to take the next step and the next. Step by step, one step at a time. That's how we learn to walk with God.

But you say, "Suppose I take the first step. What will happen next?" That's God's business. Your task and mine is to obey this day and leave the future to Him. The psalmist says our steps are "ordered by the LORD" (37:23). This day's direction is all we need. Tomorrow's instruction is of no use to us at all. George MacDonald said, "We do not understand the next page of God's lesson book; we see only the one before us. Nor shall we be allowed to turn the leaf until we have learned its lesson."

If we concern ourselves with God's will and obey each day the directions and warnings He gives, if we walk by faith and step out in the path of obedience, we will find that God will lead us through this day. As Jesus put it, "Tomorrow will worry about its own things" (Matt. 6:34). —David Roper

God knows each winding way I take,
And every sorrow, pain, and ache;
His children He will not forsake—
He knows and loves His own. —Bosch

Blessed is the person who finds out which way God is moving and then goes in that direction.

131

MY INVITATION

So what is this all going to look like? I have no clue. But I know, as sure as the ground I stand on, that God has prepared a place for us in Uganda *and* that He has prepared a wife and family that desire, more than anything, to follow God's calling, whatever... wherever... whenever. We are going to be serving the people of Uganda at the Village of Eden, that much is certain. Amber's desire, long before we met, has been to be involved on the medical side of missionary work. As mentioned earlier, it seems God has been prepping me for over a decade to help with the 'operations' management at the Village of Eden. How we get from here to there -- and exactly when -- we'll see what God does.

We met with the people who head up Helping Hands Foreign Missions and discussed an action plan in the Fall of 2013, all of which is subject to change based on our ability to raise support. The tentative plan is to begin fundraising and devise a travel schedule to start spending some extended time in Uganda as soon and often as we can.

There are a couple ways you can help, if you feel led or called to be involved in this story/journey. While I don't feel remotely comfortable 'asking' for anything from anyone, I was told by a friend to swallow my pride and at least give people the opportunity to respond, get involved, and/or offer their support in what God is doing here. He said, "Many times people, for various reasons, simply can't go like you're going... but they may want to be a part of something God is clearly 'in' like this. In being a 'sender', you give them the opportunity and blessing of becoming a stakeholder in whatever God is doing, as this is all beginning to unfold. You should at least extend the opportunity."

The simple reality is this: we will need people to partner with us in this work. If you would like to partner with what God is doing here, you can become a sponsor/supporter through Helping Hands Foreign Missions. The plane tickets to Uganda are pricey, as is ground transportation from one side of the country to the other. You can become a monthly sponsor or just send in a one-time gift -- or commit to praying for us and the work God is launching us into. If you're making a financial contribution to Helping Hands Foreign Missions via check, just indicate "Moran" in the memo line and you'll get a tax receipt at the end of the year. You can also go directly to the link below and give online through the HHFM website. You can donate frequent flyer miles, order copies of this book (or a couple others I have on the www.unlikelyinvitation.com website under) through Amazon.com to share with friends, family, your small group, or people that doubt the existence or activity of God. Anything and everything is helpful and incredibly appreciated.

When can you get involved, start giving, etc? As soon as you feel led to. If you'd like to be on a contact list, the email address or website below can be used for that. Just include your name, mailing address, and email address.

For those of you who are willing to get involved, in *any* way, not just financially, we are both grateful and humbled.

Helping Hands Foreign Missions
Attn: Long-Term Volunteers - Moran
5043 Bristol Industrial Way
Buford, GA 30518
http://helpinghandsmissions.org/store/products/
jake-and-amber-moran/

To respond in any way, visit the website or email address below:
www.unlikelyinvitation.com   unlikelyinvitation@gmail.com

FOREWORD ABOUT MY TESTIMONY

I thought it might be beneficial to share the summary version of my testimony and perhaps a couple significant landmarks in my spiritual journey for those reading this who do not know me or my experience of coming to Christ. I am so very well aware that this is in fact a journey and all journeys come with peaks and valleys. So I'll share some of those with you, as a means of encouragement -- some of my failures have been relatively hard to beat, thus if God can use me through (and despite... or maybe in spite of) my seasons of error and disobedience, I'm convinced He can use anyone. The last thing I want is for you to finish reading this and think I am 'all that'. Hopefully, you will see I'm just a guy -- with normal guy issues -- who said 'Yes' to Jesus' invitation to come and follow Him.

I should say at this point, neither in my day-to-day life nor in what I have written, do I say "God said" or "God told me" unless I have some form of confirmation that He in fact did say ___. Sometimes that comes through out-of-the-blue seemingly random confirmation via another person, or some sort of open circumstances, or a timely passage in Scripture, but there is always some form of confirmation if I ever make that sort of statement, which is relatively rare. I know that God takes His communication to mankind very seriously and it is not something I casually throw around.

And while I know that He still *speaks* to many people, I believe He will *use* no one until the white flag of unconditional surrender is raised and He is allowed to make His dwelling in a person; lock, stock, and barrel. I'll grant you this; God used Pharaoh to accomplish His ends for Moses and the Israelites, but I wouldn't recommend that route of 'being used by God'.

I attended church for most of my life, but as you'll see, it didn't do a whole lot to change who I was, just what I did or didn't do -- sometimes. What I have found to be potentially the most challenging condition within the Church as a whole, is, as D.L. Moody once wrote, "We want just enough of God for people to think we're respectable". I think this summarizes my 'attendance' record and wholly breaks the heart of God. It is my estimation that in countries where harsh persecution is not facing the Church, such as America, this is the aim of at least half of our church's congregations: just enough Jesus for a nice Christmas & Easter season, but not too much. Tell me how to have a happier family -- how to be more successful and prosperous -- just not too much of that "get out of your comfort zone and make disciples of all nations Jesus" stuff. There is either total surrender, where Jesus not only becomes Savior, but Lord/King also; or there is none.

When I got back to Georgia from visiting my family over Christmas 2012, I was going through the process of trying to re-establish some form of 'normalcy'. I had called my dish provider and cancelled my TV package with them. I know to some people, that seems downright communistic.

The reality is, plain and simple, I just came to the realization that at the end of my life, I'm 100% certain I'm not going to say, "I really wish I'd spent more time watching television." It's a vacuum that had wasted way too many hours of life already, so I cut the cord... But I was *curious* if my dish provider had also.

I have to laugh.

Honestly, I turned the TV on to see if it was truly gone-gone. That's how you know you might have a problem!

Alas! There was one channel left on, along with the music channels that the menu said would expire in three days. It was an After-Christmas-Miracle. The title displaying on the one non-music channel menu field was something called "The Greatest Story Ever Told". That's a pretty brassy title to call something, no? But it had my interest and I literally had no other options. So I hit 'enter' and low and behold -- it was Jesus. Actually it was just a semi-grungy white dude playing Jesus. I then realized Jesus' life is the greatest story ever told, so ok, I'll give you that Mr. Producer.

The scene was Judas going in to meet with the Pharisees and exchange Jesus' life for a nominal amount of silver. No big surprises with this to me; I know how this all goes down.

But God leveled me in about twenty-five seconds. I literally had the TV on for less than a minute.

As Judas walks in to meet with the Pharisees, diligently working on their scrolls, he is waived into their presence. The Pharisees, knowing who he was, asked him one question before I turned the TV off to process the gravity of the one question.

It wasn't "Where should we meet up to do the deal?"

It wasn't "How much is this going to cost us?"

It wasn't "Should this be a covert op or something we bring the battalion for?"

It wasn't "Does anyone else know you're here?"

It wasn't anything you'd expect a good payoff deal to include.

"How long have you been His friend?"

That was their first question. That absolutely wrecks me even now.

We see Judas in the background of the Gospel's as this seedy, slithering character -- he looks so obvious as the betrayer -- how do the other disciples and Jesus not oust this guy sooner?! Look at him! He's got a hood on -- and aviator sunglasses -- and a 'chester-the-molester' mustache! C'mon -- lock that dude up guys!

We have the privileged opportunity to know the end of the story as we read the middle of it. The uncomfortable reality is this: Judas was Jesus' friend, not enemy. But, there was one distinguishing characteristic about Judas that separated him from the other eleven disciples:

Judas never surrendered his will.

It was always a conditional surrender -- a deal he was in on -- nothing more. The deal didn't go as planned; Judas cashed out.

Without unconditional surrender, you might as well call me Judas Iscariot.

MY TESTIMONY

I was raised going to Catholic mass and Sunday School -- and hated it like most kids going to Catholic mass and Sunday School. Actually our Sunday School was called CCD, which I still don't know what the definition behind that acronym is. We used to think it stood for Central City Dump. Sorry "Catholics Come Home" folks; it just wasn't the desire of my heart as a young boy in grade school.

We later began going to an Episcopal church, which if Catholicism is like a black tie affair, the Episcopal Church is like a suit-and-tie affair I went through all the stuff you're supposed to go through growing up in church, some of which because I didn't know any better and some because I felt like I was supposed to. I was never really pressured to do it; I just internally felt like I should. Regardless of my desire or lack thereof, my mom did a good job of getting us to church Sunday after Sunday. There was only one big thing missing.

By age twenty-three, being in church my whole life (for the most part), I really had never opened a Bible to read for myself. If someone had asked me, "What is the Gospel?" I would have shrugged my shoulders. The church had three different hymnals in the pews, but no Bibles. Or if there were, they were -- how should I say -- crisp.

I'll skip a lot of general rebelliousness in high school and fast-forward to college. My sophomore year in college was the start of my turn around towards Christ. I had rowed all four years in high school and continued rowing at Clemson. I was kind of the 'freshman phenom' my first year, rowing varsity after only one semester; so my head was a bit inflated to say the least.

Nothing breeds pride like early success.

Even though it was just a club team, I felt like I was the rising star of the program. My second year, I lost my appetite for rowing due to a coaching change and started doing triathlons with a friend of mine. That year, I had also started dating a girl from Mississippi, who I was certain I was going to marry. Her parents loved me and we were "ga-ga" over each other. She was not only beautiful -- she absolutely lit up my life with her smile and her quirks made me roll over laughing. Things were *perfect* my first semester of my sophomore year. I felt like I was *finally* living the dream. All my hard work and patience was paying off.

But my Spring semester that year, the wheels on the bus fell off -- all six of them hitting me in the face. It was the most difficult academic semester of my tenure in college; I was involved in four or five group projects, at one point was working three different jobs, and five months into my dream relationship, my girlfriend broke up with me. My life literally fell apart about three weeks before finals week.

I found myself sitting at my desk, in my room, in my apartment, by myself, realizing I'd completely lost my carefully organized grip on life. This was the first time I heard the voice of the Holy Spirit.

From the right side of my desk, I heard a whisper that to this day I question if it was actually audible or not. It was so incredibly distinct and crystal clear. The voice seemed to almost have a tone of laughter and very simply said, "Don't you get it? You're not in control."

At that instant, I had a physical sensation like a backpack full of bricks literally fell from my shoulders. I instantly began the most joy-filled laughter I'd ever known -- and had absolutely no idea why I was laughing. I was suddenly SO HAPPY. It was the epitome of elation.

Three of my closest friends independently said something to me over the ensuing two or three months to the effect of "Hey -- what happened to you? You're like, really happy -- like, all the time. What's the story?" I had no idea what to tell them. At this point in my 'testimony' I had no idea what had happened other than *something* had definitely happened.

Over the next two years, God, in His patience (which I still don't understand), allowed me to continue to stumble and fall as 'captain of my own ship' until Sunday, March 23rd, 2003 at 9:02am.

A battle I fought for several years in college was gluttony... where I'd just eat myself sick. On Saturday, March 22nd, I had a pretty bad round with this and found myself kneeling over a toilet trying to "pull-the-trigger" -- which I couldn't do. I remember finally giving up, climbing off the floor to the sink, looking at this person in the mirror and saying, "What the heck are you doing? What... are... you... doing?"

I had been invited (and gone) several times to a church in Anderson, SC with a couple guys I had met in January, Lucas and Tony. The church was meeting in a college auditorium; it was the start of NewSpring Church. I was sitting in my Chrysler Sebring -- leather interior, a killer sound system, a sunroof, low profile tires -- and a broken twenty three year old man in the driver's seat.

Our rendezvous location was a dirt parking lot next to an old softball field, just on the outskirts of Clemson University. I would meet Lucas and Tony here and then we would carpool to church. I remember very clearly looking at my car stereo on March 23rd. It read 9:02am. I looked back at my steering wheel and felt the unmistakable presence of God staring me straight in the face, simply saying, "Are you done yet?"

I relate this experience to Revelation 3:20 where Jesus says,

"Here I stand and knock! If anyone would come and open the door, I would come in and eat with him and He with me." (NIV)

I clicked off the radio and threw my hands up in the air in an exhausted surrender, "Alright! I'm done! I'm done running my life. I clearly suck at it [I remember those exact words in case you think I'm making this up... take that 'sinners prayer']. I have no idea what I'm doing. I can't free myself from this stuff -- its one long, repeating cycle and I can't take it anymore! I have no clue what it looks like to follow You, but it *has* to be better than this! So take what's left of this life and do whatever You want, but I'm done."

Two months later I found myself in Myrtle Beach at a summer training program with The Navigators, which was effectively a nine-week crash course in seminary training -- perfect medicine for someone who didn't know where the Gospel of John was after twenty-three years in church.

I think it's worth stating, because of how a lot of people around 'the church' act about people who are new Christians, or those outside the church, with regards to sin. When I surrendered my life to Jesus, I was going to the bars in town about four nights a week. I was using all sorts of profanity. I was doing lots of things that are nowhere near 'borderline' sins; they were flagrant fouls, yet I still felt like I was a pretty good person.

What people in the church need to hear is that *no one* had to tell me the things I was doing were sinful after I surrendered my life to Christ. I literally remember the conviction of the Holy Spirit that first week and thinking, "I can't keep going out to the bars... and I need to stop swearing all the time". No one sat me down and had to tell me how to act, what words I could and couldn't use, where to go, what not to do; that's the job of the Holy Spirit. Granted, there are times when a good 'sit-down-talk' is needed, but honestly, from what I've seen, most of the people who are doing things like I mentioned that say they are Christians have never surrendered their lives to Jesus -- that's why they don't have the conviction of the Holy Spirit. They are 'cultural Christians' perhaps, ascribing to attendance, charitable works, and the like to gain perceived favor with God, but genuine followers of Jesus? Not so much.

About a year later, one of my best friends in Myrtle Beach, Ricardo, and I were sitting in the foyer of our church as part of a twenty-four-hour prayer vigil he had organized to pray for Myrtle Beach. If you had told me a year before that I'd be at a prayer vigil on a Friday night, I'd have probably told you that you were out of your mind. Well... I probably would have used much more colorful words if we're all being honest.

It's about 11:30pm Friday night and we're just talking when I begin to have this feeling/sensation that I don't quite know how to describe. The best example I think most people can connect with is the lead smock the dentist puts on you for x-rays; it felt like I was very gently being pushed down into the chair I was slouching in. I've talked with one or two other people who have had the same type of thing happen to them, and they simply describe it as the "heaviness/weight of God".

I had no idea what to make of it in the moment.

Then I felt the very clear voice of the Holy Spirit telling to stop talking -- that I was supposed to be silent. So I did.

But Ricardo kept talking. About five seconds later, it was like the Holy Spirit did an about-face and said, "Yeah – umm -- he's supposed to be silent too."

So I said to Ricardo, "Hey -- umm, I don't know what to tell you, but I feel like God wants us to be silent. I, uhh… uhh -- I don't know -- let's just pray I guess." I remember having this expression on my face like I was wearing a dunce-cap and feeling like an absolute dufus. Ricardo probably thought I was just tired of his story and wanted some silence.

So I closed my eyes and simply prayed, "What is it God?" Very spiritual right? The blackness of my eyelids started to change. Slowly, fading into focus -- as though from a distance and approaching -- seemingly on the left eyelid appeared white letters that read "IS". And then slowly, in the same fashion, on the right side appeared the white numbers "41".

Ooooki-doooki.

So I began opening my Bible to Isaiah 41. I didn't know what else IS and 41 could possibly mean?

So I flipped open to Chapter 41 -- shook my head -- and laughed.

Ricardo, who at this point, had been praying for all of fifteen seconds maybe, gives me this look like "Did you take your medicine?" I shared with him what I'd seen. Then I said, "Do you know what the first four words of Isaiah 41 are?"

He looked at me with a degree of sarcastic inquiry and said, "What?"

"Be silent before Me."

It is my estimation that God just wanted us to know that He showed up to a twenty-four-hour prayer vigil on a Friday night in Myrtle Beach, SC because He loves to show up when we least expect Him to -- even if it's at a prayer meeting.

Fast forward a year or so. I'm interviewing for a job with the YMCA in Hamilton, NJ. Without going into lots of details, God had answered some very specific prayers about leaving Myrtle Beach and I found myself interviewing for a job in the one state I swore I would *never* live in: New Jersey. While in Myrtle Beach, my day job was working at a local YMCA, while my after-hours interest centered around helping our church launch a college and young adult ministry, both of which were on my resume.

As I'm meeting different people at the Hamilton YMCA, it occurs to me I don't know a soul within a two hour radius of Hamilton, NJ. I don't have a roommate to share living expenses with, which are jacked-up expensive in New Jersey. I don't even know where a grocery store is. I am in a figurative desert. And I start to quasi-panic *during* the interviews.

I can still remember getting a tour of the front desk area. I didn't listen to a single thing the hiring manager was saying. I stood there with her behind the front desk and silently prayed as honest and deeply as I knew how to pray. "God -- just give me one," I said, "Just give me one legit, born-again Believer to encourage me here. I have no idea what I'm doing here. I'm scared and freaking out. I don't know anyone or anything around here. But if You will just give me one other Believer that can encourage me here in this desert, that will be enough."

We continued the tour and finally wrapped up. It was a cold, windy day in New Jersey, yet the hiring manager said she would walk me on out. We exit the YMCA, walk up the steps to the parking lot, and then she turns to me and says, "Look, I know I'm not supposed to say this because of HR stuff and everything, but my small group and I have been praying for several months that God would bring a Believer to fill this position. I got saved last year, born-again -- the whole bit -- and when I saw your resume with the ministry stuff, I just thought there was a chance you were the person God was sending. Look, I'm going to send you an offer this week. Just -- just let me know." I still remember standing there, absolutely blown away by what I was hearing. My silent prayer just got answered in spades.

And I turned the job down. If that's not abject disobedience, I don't know what is.

There were other factors and relationships that affected my decision greatly, but at the end of the day, it was my call to accept or reject the position. To this day, almost a decade later, I still get tears in my eyes when I share this story. I know God forgave me as I later bowed a humble and repentant heart before Him, but man -- if this speaks to you -- take the freaking job! Don't live the rest of your life with the 'What if' that comes from outright shunning of what God has gift-wrapped.

As you've read, I was married for several years before I met Amber. That chapter of my life was rough for many reasons. In trying to honor God as best as I know how, I don't feel it's probably the right, wise, or honoring thing to share much from that. I realize that leaves a huge gap in the story and leaves a lot of questions unanswered. I will simply say that while I had and have so many faults, I did not want that chapter of life to end the way it did.

And despite all the hurt and bewilderment that comes with that, I can still say God is not just good; He is awesome. He is my firm foundation and has shown His relentless love and unparalleled faithfulness in ways I could never have imagined. I hope your faith is strengthened in reading this and you are encouraged that Jesus truly is *always* working for the good of those who love Him and are called according to His purpose. You can tell Him you think His plans suck -- that He is making you feel like you are being hung out to dry -- He is not scared of your hurt or anger. We see in Scripture that He weeps with us, He sings over us, and He walks with us. What more can I ask for than a God who is near; not because He has to be, but because He wants to be.

I don't mean to end this heavy-handedly, but I really don't want anyone reading this to miss the big picture. If you are reading this and have never asked Christ to be your Savior *and* King, surrendering the keys to your castle for good, I feel it's fair to say one of two conclusions can be reached: Either everything, or at least the majority, of what I've shared is a lie -- or it's the eerie truth. And if it's the truth, then this same God I surrendered to is not only the real-deal, but His desire and delight is very simply stated: *you*, as it is/was me. God -- who is robed in light

-- desires you, as He desires me. That's both incredible and ridiculous. Why on earth would anyone not want that? Surrendering the keys to your castle is hard, but rest assured -- the *key* to His castle is way better than your castle and all its contents put together.

I was talking to a friend of mine, who is not a Christian, a little while ago and he made a comment to the effect of "clearly you and I have different ideas of who or what God is". If God is just a matter of ideology, throw all this out. Seriously -- disregard everything -- go live however you want to live because there are no eternal or lasting consequences to anything you do. *But*, if He is not just an idea, but our Creator who desires to dwell in us, then my life and my decisions have consequences I will have to answer for. Namely, "What did you choose to do with the fact that I let my boy be murdered because of your sins -- because that was the *only* way to fully heal your soul?"

My closing thought, as I evaluate my life up to this point, comes from a snippet of a conversation I overheard in the gym locker room one morning after working out. Two middle-aged guys were talking. One had just had a birthday. The big 5-0. He followed the bulk of their conversation with this seemingly errant/random comment, "Yep -- half way there."

Half way where? Half way to what? Half way to the grave, if he beats the odds and medical journals. The stats would tell him he's more likely rounding third, not sliding into second. That the sand in his hourglass of life is not halfway down and trickling into the bottom; it's got the visible funnel-pit in the middle of it and is racing to the final grain of sand.

So my thought is simply this: if you are still breathing, it is because God has not gotten enough glory for Himself out of your life yet. That may sound 'selfish' or 'narcissistic' on the surface. That's only because you don't understand the reality that *we* are the beneficiaries of the heart of God.

Surrender has become an ugly word in our culture, but let me encourage you with this: don't exit this life with the sadness of the rich young ruler. He has material prosperity, but soul poverty -- and his soul is what he's stuck with for all eternity. It ends badly for him at the end of it all -- he doesn't get to take any of his possessions or comforts with him to the grave. Emptiness or life in a place where something we see as being treasured, like gold, is seen as having such little worth that it is used to pave the streets? Can you imagine the beauty of the landscape where gold has the equivalent worth as earth's asphalt?

Of all the things I've heard talking to people in and outside Christian circles, I've never heard this:

"I surrendered my life to Jesus. Worst thing I ever did. As soon as I did, everything fell apart. Lost my job, the bank took my house, a thief broke in and stole everything I owned, and my car broke down and rolled over my dog. Single worst decision I ever made."

I've heard the polar opposite countless times.

Don't wait until you have all the answers to surrender your life to Christ; none of us will ever have all the answers.

And your hourglass is losing sand quickly.

If this book encouraged you, my prayer is that you would pay it forward and pass it along or grab another copy to give to someone you know... or a complete stranger... that looks like they might need some encouraging... because we ALL need encouragement in this journey called life.